Corporate Culture and Environmental Practice

Corporate Culture and Environmental Practice

Making Change at a High-Technology Manufacturer

Jennifer A. Howard-Grenville

Boston University, USA

Edward Elgar

Cheltenham, UK • Northampton, MA, USA

Published by
Edward Elgar Publishing Limited
Glensanda House
Montpellier Parade
Cheltenham
Glos GL50 1UA
UK

Edward Elgar Publishing, Inc.
William Pratt House
9 Dewey Court
Northampton
Massachusetts 01060
USA

A catalogue record for this book
is available from the British Library

Library of Congress Cataloguing in Publication Data

Howard-Grenville, Jennifer A., 1969–
    Corporate culture and environmental practice : making change at a high-technology manufacturer / Jennifer A. Howard-Grenville.
        p. cm.
    Includes bibliographical references and index.
    1. Industrial management—Environmental aspects. 2. Corporate culture.
I. Title.
    HD30.255.H68 2007
    658.4′083—dc22
                                                              2007001400

ISBN 978 1 84720 100 3 (cased)

Printed and bound in Great Britain by MPG Books Ltd, Bodmin, Cornwall

Contents

Acknowledgments

I am indebted to a number of colleagues and friends who, in various ways, have supported, encouraged, provided feedback on and generally believed in this book since I first thought of writing it. Without the outstanding intellectual mentorship of my cross-disciplinary dissertation committee at MIT who helped me get this started – John Ehrenfeld, John Van Maanen, Wanda Orlikowski, Maureen Scully and Leo Marx – I would not have had the foundation on which to build this version of the analysis. And without their ongoing support I would not have had the stamina to keep at it. Andy Hoffman's guidance, example and friendship have for years been a source of inspiration and help in both very pragmatic ways (reading and commenting wisely on my writing, and telling me to send it out) and in more profound ways (encouraging me to stay the course). Jim Post has been an unflappable source of advice, reason and sincere encouragement about this project and in many ways is largely responsible for helping me move it from being a 'book idea' to an actual book. John Weeks, through his own work on culture and his early comments on parts of the draft, has provided both enthusiastic encouragement and a wonderful example of cultural analysis and why it matters. Cary Coglianese and Jennifer Nash, through more recent collaboration, have helped me to think again about what goes on inside companies and put it in a larger perspective, and they have offered much support during the writing of this book. Colleagues at Boston University's School of Management – Elizabeth Craig, Kathy Kram, Tim Hall, Lloyd Baird, Aimin Yan, Bill Kahn, Fred Foulkes, Gerry Leader, CB Bhattacharya and Paul Carlile – have all played a part in having this book come out, neither too soon nor too late, and helping me along the way.

Without the openness of many 'Chipco' employees, some of whom I came to know well, others of whom I met only once or twice, and their generosity with their (limited!) time I could never have written this book. I was fortunate to participate in their world for nine months, to learn from them, and to generate my own insights into how they worked. While the analysis is my own, they were the ones who made it possible, by engaging daily with the challenges and opportunities of innovation and change.

Alan Sturmer, acquisitions editor, and all of the staff at Edward Elgar, have been a delight to work with, answering all of my questions large and small throughout the process, and making it all seem easy. I am especially grateful to three reviewers who provided very helpful feedback on the manuscript.

While the book itself was written over the last year or so, the work on which it is based has been ongoing for several years, during which many other things have happened. Three houses have been moved to, two children born, and countless early mornings, late nights, and weekends logged in an effort to rely only so much on numerous wonderful babysitters. My husband, Andrew, deserves my deepest thanks for keeping it all together, on all levels. I simply could not have done this without you. My family and extended family have all provided much needed moral and logistical support, including but not limited to several trips across the country to fill in the gaps (thanks Mom!). My children, Megan and Aidan, have been patient and flexible, have made it all worthwhile now, and continually remind me why it matters in the long run. This book is dedicated to them, with much love.

Jennifer A. Howard-Grenville
Boston, MA
December, 2006

For Aidan and Megan,
and others in their generation,
who might see things differently.

'Would it be possible for me to see something from up there?' asked Milo politely.

'You could,' said Alec, 'but only if you try very hard to look at things as an adult does.'

Milo tried as hard as he could, and, as he did, his feet floated slowly off the ground until he was standing in the air next to Alec Bings. He looked around very quickly and, an instant later, crashed back down to earth again.

'Interesting, wasn't it?' asked Alec.

'Yes, it was,' agreed Milo, rubbing his head and dusting himself off, 'but I think I'll continue to see things as a child. It's not so far to fall.'

'A wise decision, at least for the time being,' said Alec. 'Everyone should have his own point of view.'

'Isn't this everyone's Point of View?' asked Tock, looking around curiously.

'Of course not,' replied Alec, sitting himself down on nothing. 'Its only mine, and you certainly can't always look at things from someone else's Point of View. For instance, from here that looks like a bucket of water,' he said, pointing to a bucket of water; 'but from an ant's point of view it's a vast ocean, from an elephant's just a cool drink, and to a fish, of course, its home. So, you see, the way you see things depends a great deal on where you look at them from.'

(*The Phantom Tollbooth*, Norton Juster, 1961, pp. 107–8)

1. Why culture?

> The natural world does not organize itself into parables. Only people do that,
> because this is our peculiarly human method for making the world make sense.
> (Cronon, 1996: 50)

What is wrong with nature? What are the environmental ills of our day?
And what are modern corporations to do about them? On the surface, the
answers might appear straightforward. We have scientists – biologists,
climatologists, human toxicologists – to document the effects of industrial
activity on the natural world. We have laws and regulations, and agencies
who enforce them, to establish allowable and unallowable types and quantities of industrial pollutants. And we have a growing commitment among
many leading corporations to proactively reduce the environmental impact
of their operations. But we also continue to witness vehement debate
around what exactly is wrong with the environment, who is responsible, and
what ought to be done about it.

Such debates may be regarded as the norm, however, because social
groups have long differed in how they discern the natural from the unnat-
ural, normality from surprise, and safety from danger. These categorizations are the work of human cultures and they delineate what is within
their members' control from what is not, mapping the Earth's biophysical
state only imperfectly in the process. From ancient to modern times, cultures have imposed internal order by separating, purifying, and demarcat-
ing within from without (Douglas, 1966). And, throughout time, cultural
groups have differed in how they make these distinctions, and with what
consequences.

Organizational cultures are no exception. While they may be less colorful
than the rituals of ancient tribes, the patterns of action and language of the
modern corporation purge and purify nonetheless. Certain problems are
selected for attention, certain solutions invoked. The environmental impacts
of industrial activity are real, to be sure, but choices of which environmental impacts constitute problems and how to mitigate them are shaped by a
host of factors including, critically, those internal to organizations.

In this book, I turn a company inside out in an effort to understand its
nature. What environmental ills does it seek to address? What does it do
about them? This book is about the internal norms and practices that shape

one company's attention to and actions on environmental issues. It explores the data-driven, engineering-oriented culture of a high-tech manufacturer and the actions of a group who sought to better integrate environmental considerations into such a culture. While it draws attention to considerable and fundamental gaps between the company's mainstream modes of work and the demands placed by environmental issues, it also explores an emergent process of change that occurred as those advancing the environmental considerations gradually moved them closer to the core concerns of the organization over a six-year period. In the end, then, this book is also about getting environmental issues 'in' to a company, not through wholesale organizational culture change as some predict and wish for,[1] but through gradual, cumulative actions that both attach the new issues to existing cultural understandings so they become legitimate problems and, at the same time, expose the core culture's blind spots.

The analysis is based on a nine-month participant observation study of 'Chipco',[2] a major US-based semiconductor manufacturer whose primary products are computer 'chips.' I focus on two groups within Chipco, 'Tech' and 'EnviroTech,'[3] and their interactions. Tech is a 1500-person technology development group, responsible for developing new manufacturing equipment and procedures that enable the production of faster, more powerful chips. EnviroTech, a much smaller group, was formed within a few years of my study to work with members of Tech to reduce the environmental impact of future manufacturing processes. By following the actions and interactions in their day-to-day work, and the larger cultural meanings attached to such actions, I develop a new, cultural perspective on the motivations for a company's environmental practices. This cultural perspective complements and extends current scholarship that seeks to explain how firms act on environmental issues, and what motivates them to do so.

Research on corporate environmental management has offered many explanations for why companies choose to take the actions they do on environmental issues. Work in the strategic and economic traditions emphasizes the potential competitive advantage companies gain by reducing pollution and waste (Porter and Van der Linde, 1995) or by developing capabilities that enable them to learn about and effectively respond to stakeholder demands on environmental issues (Sharma and Vredenburg, 1998; Marcus and Nichols, 1999). Work in the sociological tradition draws attention to how the 'rules of the game' defining acceptable corporate environmental practice shift over time in response to the expectations and actions of a large number of actors – governments, non-governmental organizations, industry associations, and the general public (Hoffman, 1999). Companies both actively shape and respond to such shifts in rules (Howard-Grenville *et al.*, 2007). Several scholars have drawn attention to the range of external pressures that might contribute to the actions that individual companies take. Regulatory and economic conditions, as well as social demands and norms, matter, but different aspects of these are more or less salient for individual companies (Gunningham *et al.*, 2003). Finally, several accounts remind us that the environment itself ought to directly influence a company's actions as biophysical resources impose both short- and long-term constraints on a company's ability to carry out its work (Gladwin *et al.*, 1995; Hart, 1995).

Common to all of these explanations is a focus on how external conditions – economic, regulatory, social, environmental, and combinations of these – create opportunities (and threats) that might induce certain actions on the part of firms. Also common, until recently, is a silence about what goes on within companies that might shape their perceptions of these conditions, the opportunities or threats that they pose, and the actions they might take as a result. Recent research demonstrates that companies act differently on environmental issues even when they face similar external conditions and pressures (Prakash, 2000; Gunningham *et al.*, 2003), suggesting that even the most nuanced assessment of external pressures will offer an incomplete explanation. Meanwhile, several scholars have turned inward, to explore how managers' commitments, perceptions, and leadership influence how they interpret external pressures for environmental performance (Coglianese and Nash, 2001; Andersson and Bateman, 2000; Sharma, 2000; Forbes and Jermier, 2002).

This book picks up this inward focus, but uses a cultural lens and in-depth observational data to articulate what shaped perceptions of environmental issues at Chipco, focusing first on the core work of the group asked to incorporate new environmental demands. By contrasting the prevailing cultural norms and practices with those being introduced with the new demands, we see that managers' perceptions and interpretations of environmental issues need not be regarded as idiosyncratic. They may be highly consistent with their work and that of their organizations. Furthermore, a focus on culture and interaction draws attention to how cultural meanings can act as a constraint to change, but, importantly, also an opportunity for making change from within. The message of the book for scholars is that close attention to the internal workings of a firm can shed considerable light on its decisions to undertake particular environmental actions. For managers and those seeking change within companies, the book is a call to deeply understand the cultures in which they operate and to use this knowledge to build change from the inside out.

Before elaborating on these implications, a vignette from Chipco offers an illustration. It demonstrates that the most critical and urgent environmental issues inside Chipco were not those that were most stringently regulated, subject to vocal opposition, or whose resolution was economically attractive, nor were they necessarily those that had the greatest impact on the natural environment. Indeed, none of the standard regulatory, scientific, social or economic drivers of environmental practice could, alone or together, fully explain Chipco's actions on particular issues. The critical environmental issues for Chipco were those that challenged the company's capacity to control and predict the development of its manufacturing technology, considered a key core competence. Maintaining internal order, the work of an organization's culture, strongly shaped which environmental issues gained attention and the actions taken to resolve them.

CONSTRUCTING A CRISIS: THE 'CLEAN AIR' PROJECT

Each month, a group of Chipco managers and engineers from EnviroTech, Tech and other groups formally met to decide on courses of action to mitigate the environmental impacts of the company's planned chip manufacturing processes. Described as strategic, these meetings of the 'EnviroCouncil'[4] were attended by invitation only. Members were there to do work; they listened to the data presented, analyzed trends and constraints, chose among alternatives, and, as a group, formally ratified decisions. The goals of the EnviroCouncil were to preempt environmental problems before they happened, to deliver solutions that consistently improved the environmental performance of each successive manufacturing process generation, and to build these solutions into the very fabric of the new manufacturing technologies. At a place like Chipco, where a new manufacturing process generation and its significantly new technology and equipment base is rolled out every two years, this is a tall order.

Toward the end of one three-hour EnviroCouncil teleconference, an engineer presented air emissions data for newly selected manufacturing equipment. He concluded by emphasizing that no solution had been identified that would reduce these emissions with the required 95 percent efficiency and also handle a second highly flammable gas present in the equipment's exhaust stream. Always entrained to the pacing of new manufacturing generations, he reminded the group that any solution had to be ready for high-volume manufacturing operation within ten months.

Silence fell over the conference room as the engineer wrapped up his presentation, and for a few moments the phone line registered none of the usual remarks or questions. 'People are picking themselves off the floor right now,' one manager quipped. After their initial silence, EnviroCouncil members began to voice their assessments of the issue. 'This is the biggest environmental problem we have ever faced,' commented one. Another, with a flair for hyperbole, made a reference to a well-known environmental catastrophe.

What was the problem? As a threat to the natural environment, the magnitude of the projected air emissions were far from catastrophic. They were well below any absolute regulatory limits on hazardous air emissions,[5] but exceeded Chipco's internally established goal for such emissions by a factor of 20. Meeting the goal retained Chipco's flexibility to make future chemical changes within its manufacturing facilities without undergoing additional time-consuming regulatory reviews. And as speed and the ability to optimize the manufacturing process at all times were of critical importance to Chipco's success, this air emissions goal was considered non-negotiable. Similarly nonnegotiable was Tech's decision to adopt the new equipment as it promised improved process performance. 'We can't challenge this selection, we've got to make it work,' urged one EnviroCouncil member.

And make it work they did. Instead of representing their concerns to others in terms of air emission quantities, members of the EnviroCouncil created a chart that depicted the maximum possible manufacturing output that would keep factories within the emission goal. If an adequate environmental solution was not found, the chart made clear, the factories would be limited to an embarrassingly small maximum chip output. As one manager noted and communicated widely, it was the 'first time the environmental implications are the biggest technical hurdle to bringing [new manufacturing equipment] in.' Indeed, this got attention within Tech. A work group was formed immediately and managed to secure support for the project from Tech's senior management. Tech engineers were assigned to work on the project alongside environmental specialists, and money was obtained from the Tech budget.

The group left no stone unturned as they worked on technical approaches to reduce emissions from the prototype equipment and then searched for a treatment system that would destroy the remaining air emissions. Within four months they had developed a technical solution that was fully integrated with the new process equipment, simultaneously beating the schedule and the emissions goal. This was a refreshing change from earlier environmental projects that had been plagued by much more complex technical and operational problems than originally anticipated, and that sometimes lagged the deployment of the process equipment they were designed to serve. One environmental engineer offered a simple explanation for the 'Clean Air'[6] project's success: 'it was the first time we treated an [environmental device] like a process tool.'[7]

A sense of crisis, the opportunity to rise to a seemingly insurmountable technical challenge to remove a potential constraint on manufacturing, and the need to do it all in a very short period of time are standard experiences for those engaged in technical work at Chipco. The Clean Air project was, or at least became, a problem of this type. Depicted as a critical technical challenge that would ultimately limit manufacturing, the problem invoked the focused, disciplined technical problem-solving that was the hallmark of work at Tech. The environmental 'crisis' was averted. The offensive air emissions had been cut to well below the internally set goal. But where had they gone? While the Clean Air solution removed the harmful chemical from the air exhaust, it transferred it to a liquid waste stream, which was then treated and dried to produce a solid waste that was shipped to landfill.

Those engaged in environmental work at Chipco recognized this as a suboptimal solution. One member of the EnviroCouncil reflected a few months later that there was a 'fair amount of complexity and cost associated with treating the "lifecycle"' of the chemical in the current way (from the process input gas, to the exhaust gas, to the liquid form and finally solid form). But, he added, 'it looks like [the process input gas] is here to stay. The question for the next five years is whether it will be possible to capture the [the chemical] in gas phase and recycle it into [the process input gas] without going through the whole lifecycle.' This question would require a fundamental redesign of the environmental treatment approach. Work on such a recycling system did not fit the predominant modes and forms of manufacturing process development work. It stood outside the time cycle on which this work turned, bucking the relentless two-year 'treadmill' on which new manufacturing technologies were developed. And it failed to resonate as urgent enough to warrant broad action. As one manager explained '[Chipco] tends to focus on things that limit performance, the whole corporate psyche is around problem-solving.' And, with the immediate Clean Air crisis averted, the problem was considered solved.

CULTURES AND CRISES

The Clean Air project illustrates why it is so problematic to talk in absolutes about corporate environmental problems and the practices adopted to address them. The problems themselves are at least partially defined internally. Here the air emissions problem – its nature and size – was intimately tied to Chipco's desire for manufacturing flexibility and speed. The solutions, similarly, address the problems that are felt, and likely invoke organizational norms that are much deeper and broader than simply those governing environmental practice. At Chipco, the Clean Air solution was a Tech solution – it removed constraints on future manufacturing, matched the development cycle for the new manufacturing generation, and came about through the focused application of brute technical force.

While the internal norms and practices of the company mattered a great deal to how the problem was constructed and how it was resolved, external factors clearly mattered also. Without a regulatory framework in place that allowed facilities greater flexibility to make process changes if air emissions were below a certain threshold, exceeding Chipco's emissions goal would not have been so consequential. Without a competitive environment in the industry that rewarded firms who were first to market with chips produced on state-of-the-art manufacturing equipment, Chipco's need for timely manufacturing technology development would not have been so urgent. Ultimately, however, these external pressures were interpreted and prioritized through cultural categories and understandings present within the firm.

Culture is a pattern of meanings (Geertz, 1973) that are represented and recreated through the actions and communications of members of a group. These patterns do not simply arise arbitrarily; they are developed as a group 'solve[s] its problems of external adaptation and internal integration' (Schein, 1992). In other words, cultures evolve from their members' interactions with the outside world and with each other. Cultures offer their members ready-at-hand categories for problems (Douglas, 1966) and repertoires of 'strategies for action' (Swidler, 1986) that are particularly suited to solving the problems recognized by the culture. But they are also historical, adaptive and emergent social phenomenon (Weeks and Galunic, 2003), that are neither perfectly nor immediately responsive to the outside world, nor fully designed by individuals. Cultures take on complex, multifaceted lives of their own; members of a group tend to recreate or, less frequently, alter them through their actions, though not all with the same effect or for the same reasons. Inherent in any culture is a certain amount of inertia and a certain amount of unintended consequence. This paradoxical relationship between human agency and cultural evolution is summed up in the observation that culture is 'created by intentional activities but is not an intended project' (Giddens, 1984: 27).

What does this mean for the actions observed at Chipco? How can it be used to understand company's environmental practices? First, it implies that cultural meanings and the actions they are associated with are typically much broader and deeper than those that might be attached only to environmental practices. In other words, a company's culture evolves from its entire spectrum of interactions with the external world, as well as from choices about how it is going to organize internally to cope with these interactions. Environmental practices are but one of a host of external interactions companies engage in, and they are a relatively recent set of concerns.

This suggests that the cultures of established companies are typically more or less 'in place' and the important implication for environmental management is how (and how effectively) the cultural apparatus – meanings, categories, and the strategies for action they support – is mobilized in the face of these relatively new issues.

A second implication is that a full explanation for a company's environmental activities cannot come from external or internal factors alone. Broad external conditions, such as those defining the economic, market, or social conditions an industry or company faces, contribute directly to how a company experiences pressures for environmental management. These very external conditions may also contribute over time to the development and evolution of a company's culture. But the finding that companies in the same industry, subject to similar external pressures, often adopt quite different environmental management approaches (Prakash, 2000; Gunningham *et al.*, 2003), reminds us that internal factors have their own influence.

Internally, the company's culture serves to sort and prioritize external pressures into specific problems to be acted upon, and offer modes of action through which appropriate solutions can be sought. Indeed, the categorization of problems by a company itself can, at times, contribute to how they are perceived and portrayed externally (Edelman *et al.*, 1999; Hoffman, 1999; Gunningham *et al.*, 2003). This suggests a more recursive and reciprocal understanding of internal and external motivators for environmental practice, but one which recognizes companies themselves (or, more accurately, members of the companies) as active agents in the formulation of environmental problems and solutions that suit them. Figure 1.1 captures the conceptual relationships between these external and internal factors.

The emphasis in this book is on the internal factors, and specifically the cultural factors, that shape companies' actions on environmental issues, for the internal factors have been given considerably less systematic empirical attention and their contribution to environmental practice and performance is consequently often overlooked. They serve as both a source of inertia and resistance to change and, significantly, a potentially important lever for change as insiders can exploit cultural meanings for new ends.

A CULTURAL PERSPECTIVE ON CORPORATE ENVIRONMENTAL PRACTICE

By mapping out the cultural terrain within a single company, one can begin to understand how certain external conditions are perceived by its members – as threats or opportunities, issues or non-issues. At Chipco the culture itself was strongly informed by the nature of the company's core

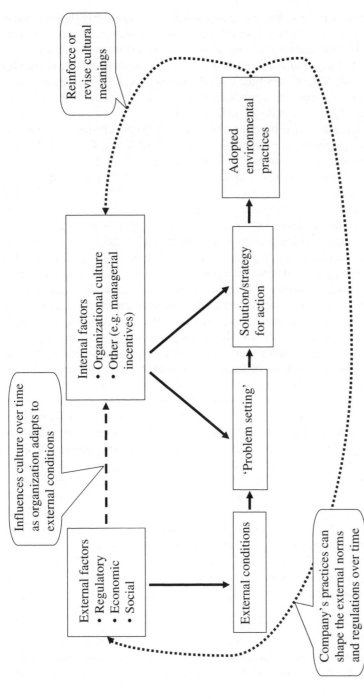

Figure 1.1   Relationships between external and internal factors shaping corporate environmental practice

work, developing and operating exquisitely precise and highly predictable high-tech manufacturing technologies. Those working on new, less pre-dictable environmental issues found their problems treated with some sus-picion, and their solutions an imperfect fit with the dominant strategies for action. Nonetheless, over time and across repeated projects they began to appropriate the cultural apparatus of the core groups to better advance environmental issues and gain action on them.

How general are the findings from Chipco? What can they tell us about how other companies might act on environmental issues? What can they tell us about making change within a dominant culture? Perhaps no other company works quite like Chipco. Indeed, others set measurable goals, aggressively pursue them, and connect these goals to the company's overall strategy and operational needs. But few companies, I suspect, focus quite so relentlessly as Chipco does on such things. For in this industry, the emphasis on paced innovation is not simply a cultural norm; it is a Law. Moore's Law observes and predicts the doubling of transistor density – the number of components on a given size of chip and a proxy for its comput-ing power – every two years. It is the reason computers and other electronic devices have seen such vast increases in capability, and such vast decreases in size and power requirements over the years. And it is the key reason for Chipco's focus on the timely development and deployment of new manufacturing technologies, and a plethora of practices and norms that support this. As one Tech engineer noted 'if there's no new process, there's no Chipco.'

With this focus on planned, predictable, yet extremely challenging tech-nology development, Chipco's normal mode of work stands in stark con-trast to its experience of work on environmental issues which often resisted planning, belied close prediction, and were not simply technical. It is for this very reason that Chipco presents a valuable extreme case (Eisenhardt, 1989; Pettigrew, 1990), perhaps amplifying differences between its core work and culture and the demands brought in addressing environmental issues. Like any extreme case, however, more general implications can be identified that apply to other companies. Key among these are that a com-prehensive understanding of internal norms and practices is essential for outsiders seeking to understand particular courses of action taken by com-panies on environmental issues, as it is for those inside a company seeking to influence change.

Inside and Out

The first implication is that internal factors matter a great deal in how a company acts on environmental issues. External factors – like regulation, social pressures, scientific information and resource and competitive pressure – clearly matter too, but they tell only part of a complex story. It may be difficult or impossible to predict the actions of a given company even if one understood in detail the external conditions to which it was subject. A focus on organizational culture is an extension of recent efforts to elaborate internal factors, like managerial perceptions, individual values, and managerial commitment (Andersson and Bateman, 2000; Egri and Herman, 2000; Sharma, 2000; Coglianese and Nash, 2001; Bansal, 2003), that shape company's decision making and actions on environmental issues.

But culture offers a better construct on which to build an argument for the importance of internal factors to environmental practice than do some of the other constructs that may simply be empirically derived. Like these other constructs, culture draws attention to the internal construction of external pressures – without denying that external pressures and issues have a life of their own – but it also offers well established theoretical explanations for these constructions. Culture is, in some sense a 'root cause' of manager's perceptions and contributes at least partially to the values and commitments they express at work. Manager's interpretations of environmental issues will differ, to be sure, with their own personal values and affiliations, but as anthropologist Mary Douglas reminds us, culture is not entirely negotiable (1978).

Culture – as patterns of meaning and associated actions – captures the significance of daily organizational practices, and the work that is being accomplished through those practices. By focusing on a company's members' experiences of daily work, as I do in Chapters 4 and 5, one can develop a more holistic picture of assumptions about or understandings of the physical world, knowledge, time and individual interaction that are bound up in work practice and that importantly influence interpretations of environmental issues and actions on them. Manager's incentives and commitments are important, but cannot usefully be stripped from the context – both organizational and external – in which they are developed and defended. Close, comprehensive attention to culture is key to making sense of specific interpretations and actions on environmental issues. It connects the work of the company, the manifestations of this work in its daily practices and norms, and understandings of the natural and nonnatural world that are consistent with these, to the particular problems that are selected for attention and the actions taken to address them.

In his book about the influence of broad institutional and social norms on changes in corporate environmental practice, Hoffman points out that

To profess, as many today do, that industry is finally seeing the light is to argue that the light has always been there to see. In fact it has not. How companies

define their responsibility toward the environment is a direct reflection of how
we, as a society, view the environmental issue and the role of business in responding to it. (Hoffman, 2001: 22)

The cultural view developed here adds that the light, changing as it does
with shifts in the external 'rules of the game,' is not seen equally by all
who are exposed to it. A company's culture acts as a kind of window,
projecting the light in distinct ways within the organization. To understand
a company's environmental practices, we must attempt to see *their* light.

Culture, Consequence and Change

A second implication from the Chipco analysis speaks more directly to the
work on organizational culture and change. While a number of in-depth
studies hold up a mirror to the meanings – positive, negative, shared and
disjointed – associated with particular organizational cultures and explore
their consequences,[8] few have focused on the consequences of an organization's culture for its actions toward the outside world. By doing so, this
analysis captures some of the pressures for adaptation that an organization's culture is subject to, and draws attention to the different times scales
and dynamics associated with external demands and internal processes.
External events can trigger sudden calls for revision in how a company acts
on issues such as those related to the natural environment. Companies may
make immediate responses to such trigger events, but their core culture
likely adjusts much more slowly (if at all). While we know that cultures can
change, we also know that they often do not change easily, and are encumbered by inertia due to the fact that their very existence is owed to the
distributed yet patterned communications and actions of a large number of
individuals. Exploring cultural patterns of resistance, moments of opportunity, and what comes of these, as external demands buffet a culture is
an important addition to the repertoire of studies that focus on how an
organization's culture shapes insiders' experiences.

    This book also demonstrates that organizational culture can shape atten-
tion and action on external issues in nuanced ways. As many have pointed
out, organizational cultures are rarely monolithic, nor static (Schein,
1996; Martin, 2002; Gregory, 1983). Multiple, perhaps conflicting, systems
of meaning operate within many cultures (Meyerson and Martin, 1987;
Martin, 2002), suggesting that cultures, or the subcultures within them,
offer many possible ways that problems are set and many possible strategies
for action. Whose interpretations win? Which strategies for action trump
others? The literature on culture has remained relatively silent on questions
of power within cultures and between subcultures, but groups whose work

is considered central to the work of the organization as a whole wield disproportionate power (Hickson *et al.*, 1971; Hinings *et al.*, 1974) and may wield disproportionate influence over how problems are set and how they are solved.

Indeed, the Chipco analysis suggests that those doing environmental work were 'pulled' toward representing their concerns using the language and norms of Tech. But at the same time, environmental issues moved at least a little closer to Chipco's core concerns. By following how particular projects were approached over time, and shifts in how successfully they were implemented, the Chipco analysis reinforces the observation that members of a culture are not passive 'cultural dopes,' (Swidler, 1986: 277) but are active, skillful users of culture. They are capable of holding multiple interpretations, having multiple intentions (Howard-Grenville, 2005), and knowingly appropriating cultural norms and practices to suit these. While culture is not entirely negotiable, it is not immutable either. Observing the interactions of two very different groups – one dominant and central, and one small and advancing new issues – and following these over time, as I do in Chapter 6, draws attention to the contours and contradictions within organizational cultures, and how these shape opportunities and barriers for change.

Making Environment Matter

A final key implication from the Chipco analysis is for the practice of environmental management. To gain attention to and get action on such issues one must become a student of the mainstream organizational culture, or at least the culture of a dominant group, deeply understanding the opportunities and constraints it presents for advancing these issues. To make environmental issues the legitimate concerns of all, they must be understood as problems for all, or at least problems for some other powerful group. And to gain action on them one should solicit not necessarily (or not only) those who are personally committed to the issues but those who are committed to the organization as a whole, and experienced in navigating its culture. These are the people who can skillfully and pragmatically deploy the strategies for action that are trusted and essential to advance the issues. Chapter 6 explores the craft of 'issue selling' (Dutton and Ashford, 1993) when faced with influencing the attention and action of a dominant group within a culture. By learning over time and across repeated interactions about the problems and concerns of another group, groups and individuals can gradually acquire the ability to sell new issues in culturally compatible ways.

Putting a problem in terms that animate the concerns of a dominant group necessarily limits the range of interpretations and actions that are possible, which perhaps explains an observed conservative bias in advancing new issues (Dutton *et al.*, 2001). Ultimately it also limits how authentically and thoroughly the new considerations are integrated into the organization's culture. Pragmatic strategies of compromise can be precursors to cooption, especially if those advancing new issues become increasingly familiar with and comfortable with the language of a more powerful group (Meyerson and Scully, 1995). But the threat of selling out must be balanced with the need – especially in a strong organizational culture like Chipco's – for 'selling in,' getting these issues onto the mainstream agenda gradually, and accumulating the capacity to have greater influence, ultimately perhaps shifting or expanding the nature of problems that are attended to and the repertoire of strategies for action within the company.

A MAP OF THE BOOK

In the next chapter I provide some more detail on Chipco, first as a culture by introducing the reader to Chipco in the way I was introduced and next as the subject of this study by providing an overview of the research methodology. The latter half of Chapter 2 paints the 'bigger picture' of environmental practices in the semiconductor manufacturing industry by giving an overview of environmental interactions, economic and technological trends, and social and regulatory pressures, which provide a backdrop against which Chipco's actions on particular environmental issues can be assessed. A theoretical framework for the subsequent analysis is offered in Chapter 3. I first reiterate that 'nature' and the 'environment' are at least partially culturally constructed and explore the implications of this by considering two prominent academic explanations for corporate environmental practice and their respective gaps. In the remainder of Chapter 3 I use the literature on organizational culture and subcultures to argue that cultures generate affinities for certain types of problems and certain valued strategies for action. I conclude Chapter 3 by suggesting that interactions between subcultures or organizational groups with different amounts of power will lead to contestation of problem setting and strategies for action and will shape efforts to sell issues to a dominant subculture or group.

The core cultural analysis of Chipco is presented in Chapters 4, 5 and 6. Chapter 4 describes in detail the work of Tech, the dominant manufacturing technology development group, and understandings that accompany this work. Chapter 5 focuses on those doing environmental work, primarily EnviroTech, and parallels Chapter 4 in describing the environmental work and understandings that accompany it, and drawing comparisons and contrasts with Tech. Chapter 6 switches the focus from the work and culture of different groups to how these groups interacted over time on specific projects. Drawing on an analysis of seven specific projects over a six year period, it demonstrates a shift in how the environmental issues were represented and acted upon over time, and explores reasons for this shift. Finally, Chapter 7 concludes with implications of attention to organizational culture and environmental practice for theory on corporate environmental management, for theory on culture and culture change, for employees working on issues that fit uneasily with a dominant organizational culture, and for environmental policy.

NOTES

1. Despite early literature on environmental management that predicted transformations within companies as they adopted increasingly enlightened environmental practices (Hunt and Auster, 1990; Roome, 1992; Gladwin *et al.*, 1995; Shrivastava, 1995) such changes have been slow in coming, at best, and seldom has attention to environmental issues radically transformed how organizations operate (Halme, 2002; Newton, 2003).
2. The company named 'Chipco' throughout this book and its subsidiary 'EnviroTech' are pseudonymous. Characterizations of the companies here referred to as 'Chipco' and 'EnviroTech' are my own and are derived from my research and data collection. They are not intented to reflect observations on any actual company bearing the word 'Chipco' or 'EnviroTech' in its name. Any similarities between the fictitious 'Chipco' or 'EnviroTech' in this book and a real company are coincidental and unintentional. All personal and group names have been disguised in this book to protect the identity of individuals and the company.
3. All group names are pseudonyms.
4. 'EnviroCouncil' is also a pseudonym.
5. For comparison, more than 120 US manufacturing facilities emitted at least Chipco's projected quantity of the class of air pollutants that this emission fell into, and several of them emitted more than ten times this projected amount. (US Environmental Protection Agency 1999).
6. This and other project names used in the book are pseudonyms.
7. 'Tool' is a generic term used within the industry to refer to the complex manufacturing equipment.
8. Exemplars include Kunda, 1992; Smith, 1990; and Weeks, 2004.

2.   Getting to know Chipco

Not knowing your acronyms at Chipco is a CLB . . . career limiting behavior.
                                                           Chipco trainer

Learning any new company takes time. And learning how a company learns about new issues and acts on them takes, well, more time. In this chapter I introduce Chipco as I was introduced to it by reflecting on my initial encounter with the culture, and outlining larger themes that are explored more fully in the book. I then discuss how I learned about the culture by describing my method of participant observation. In the last part of the chapter I answer a question that might be on the minds of some readers. Why study the environmental actions of a chip manufacturer? Aren't they one of the cleanest manufacturing industries around? I outline the environmental impacts related to semiconductor manufacturing and provide an overview of the economic conditions, technological and regulatory trends, and social pressures that contribute to how members of this industry experience environmental issues. This sets the stage for developing a cultural view of environmental practice in Chapter 3, and analyzing Chipco's interpretations and actions on specific environmental issues in the subsequent chapters.

ENCOUNTERING CHIPCO CULTURE

Few January days dawned bright and sunny at my Chipco location, and this Monday morning was no exception. At 7:30 a.m., it was still dark and drizzling steadily as I arrived at a low, sprawling office building for New Employee Orientation, or NEO. I presented myself at the building's security desk and was handed a three-inch binder of documents, then directed to a windowless conference room. Patty, a 'Chipco University' instructor, firmly directed me and others to fill out forms and step into an adjoining room to have pictures taken for our employee badges. Coffee, juice, donuts and bagels were laid out on a long table at the back of the conference room but Patty shooed away anyone who had not yet had their picture taken. There was a procedure to follow, and it was strictly, if gently, enforced.

As my 65 or so fellow travelers settled into their seats, I flipped open the binder and found my NEO 'passport.' The first page was a traveler profile, with blank spaces where I could fill in my employee number, job assignment, manager's name, site address, mailstop, building/pole number, telephone number, and email address. The following page listed some of these identifiers, but all were incorrect because they referred to my manager's out of state location. Later that afternoon I would make my way to the cubicle that would be home for nine months, building R1, third floor, pole number C14. Hundreds of identical 8ft × 9ft cubicles filled the third floor of R1, lettered and numbered like stalls in a parking garage for ease of navigation.

Dave, Patty's co-instructor, got the NEO class going shortly after 8 a.m. Why were we here? Dave laid out the objectives for the next six hours: NEO would provide each of us with an action plan, prepare us for our first one-on-one meeting with our manager, and give us a list of ARs for the first few days at work. Patty interrupted from the back of the room, suggesting that new hires would not know what 'AR' stood for, and Dave cracked 'not knowing your acronyms at Chipco is a CLB.' He paused and added, 'career limiting behavior.' AR, he went on to explain, stands for Action Required. Part of Chipco's nomenclature for parsing out work, an AR is something owned by an individual, and tracked by that individual's peers. When completed, an AR represents work output.

Throughout the day Dave orchestrated a fast-moving sequence of his own presentations on Chipco's values and organizational structure, interspersed with short videos on everything from the CEO's welcome message to office safety, and a presentation and question session with an ESM (executive staff member). The tone was serious and professional, peppered with the right mix of jokes and facts to keep people alert. Apparently the first offering of a new revision of the NEO material, the class nonetheless came off as carefully sequenced and timed, perhaps due to Dave and Patty's experience of training 100 new employees per week for most of the previous year. Even our lunch break was a part of the performance. We first lined up to present identification verifying employment eligibility to one of several young women from human resources; only then were we allowed near the buffet table and sandwiches.

Small talk was permitted once we'd completed more paperwork at our seats during the 'working lunch.' Anyone starting work that week at any of Chipco's four major (and several smaller) 'campuses' in the state had been required to attend. A nurse who would work night shift at one of the factories, a physics Ph.D graduate from the Midwest who took an engineering job after a rejection from McKinsey, a software programmer who would work for Chipco's small but growing 'content' division, and a 15-year veteran of the semiconductor industry who would work as a manufacturing technician were among the class. We all heard the same videotaped message from the CEO, stressing that Chipco is a goal oriented organization that demands its people make good decisions quickly. Some messages were reiterated by Dave: work at Chipco is disciplined, but taking risks is rewarded, individuals are responsible for their own success and failure. The CEO's video ended with him looking straight into the camera, and saying, 'something new was added to Chipco today – you. You have the opportunity to have an influence – seize it.'

By 2 p.m. I felt cross-eyed. The run of three short videos in the darkened conference room immediately after lunch left many in the audience flagging. One video was a very staid newscast style piece in which two lawyers discussed sexual harassment, a second urged us to be fanatical about safety and taught us about office ergonomics, and a third reviewed the history of Chipco's operations in the state. Dave, perhaps mentally noting that they might try those videos at a different time for the next week's class, stood up and, with the energy and good cheer of an MC at a wedding urging everyone to get up and dance, closed the class by telling us to heed a Chipco founder's advice: 'don't be encumbered by history – go off and do something wonderful.' Passport binders in hand, we filed out to find our buildings, navigate the pole numbers, and locate our cubicles.

The day after NEO I learned that going off and doing something wonderful at Chipco wasn't a call for unfettered creativity. I needed a work plan, and my work plan needed to have clear, succinct targets and expected completion dates, or ECDs, for each. Furthermore, my work plan had to serve the goals of my group and organization. If it fit on one page, with elements numbered and displayed in a tabular format, I gathered that would be a distinct plus. Having discussed the objectives of my work for the next several months with my manager, I put together what I thought was adequate.

My manager took me and my work plan down to the cafeteria, where virtually all meetings between two or more people took place to avoid overcrowding the cubicles. We met with a manager from the manufacturing technology development ('Tech') organization, and at the first sight of my work plan he snapped that my outlined objectives were 'vague and unmeasurable.' As he went through the plan and circled words that he claimed he didn't understand, he told me that he had to see specific statements with measurable outcomes and target dates so that he would be able to 'hold my feet to the fire.' I was intimidated but realized that the only way to counter his behavior was to be direct and assertive right back, so I told him what I planned to do as concisely as I could and he flipped over the sheet of paper my work plan was written on and told me to write it down as I'd said it. Action words counted. Actions could be tracked and measured.

CHIPCO CULTURE AND THE ENVIRONMENT

Two days in an organization does not make one an expert on the culture, but early cues are important signifiers of how things are done. After nine months of full-time participant observation, and months of analysis of my field notes, I came to an understanding of the Chipco culture that is related in this book, and that puts into perspective what is culturally significant about those early days. Chipco, as one senior manager observed, is a very 'literal organization.' Goals are set, ARs assigned, data gathered. Experiments are performed, deliverables met, results obtained. There are rules to be followed, and they are strictly, if often tacitly, enforced.

Measurement is all important, for it provides a clear and clean tool for assessing progress made and progress still to come. Technical challenges, and those who solve them, enjoy high status at Chipco. The focus is on making the technology work – producing new, advanced manufacturing processes that in turn produce faster, higher performance chips. Time is a critical resource. Chipco develops and deploys a new generation of manufacturing processes every two years, and its engineers work under an almost continual sense of crisis.

In this culture, environmental issues often were an uneasy fit. Data was harder to come by, specific targets harder to set, and even harder to meet. Perceptions of outsiders always mattered. Narrowly technical solutions did not always appease regulators, communities, or activists. Those working on environmental issues saw themselves as 'trying to balance a technical solution with a political problem.' Whether they believed in the issue at hand or not, they recognized it as an issue nonetheless. One manager noted about a specific environmental problem, 'it's a force – whether its real or not – it still has to be worked.' And 'working' a problem increasingly took the form of working a technology problem as the Clean Air project demonstrated in Chapter 1.

In an organization where vague and unmeasurable concepts are suspect, where an orientation to immediate results makes individual action and accountability paramount, how were environmental issues treated? And how did those working on them move them, albeit gradually, from the fringes of corporate concern to somewhere closer in? These questions are taken up in Chapters 4, 5 and 6 where I draw on my observations of the nine months following NEO to consider how organizational culture shaped attention and action on environmental issues at Chipco. Here I turn to a description of my method – how I trained my attention and action on these questions.

THE SETTING AND THE STUDY

Understanding a culture, a pattern of meanings and actions, implies sharing 'firsthand the environment, problems, background, language, rituals and social relations' of a group of people (Van Maanen, 1988: 3). Fieldwork – using techniques of extended participant-or nonparticipant-observation, interviewing, and collection of artifacts and documents – is the term most often used to refer to this activity, and ethnography – a written representation of the culture – its product (Van Maanen, 1988). As in many corporate settings, extended access to Chipco was only possible through formal membership. Members of Chipco were themselves trying to understand how to better address environmental issues associated with new manufacturing processes and, with an educational background that enabled me to understand the technical aspects of semiconductor manufacturing as well as the conditions and constraints of organizational change, I entered into a nine-month graduate student internship intended to study – for the benefit of both sides – how these issues were acted upon at Chipco.

During this time, I worked with those directly involved in assessing environmental impacts of existing and new process technologies, defining environmental goals, and planning and implementing procedural and equipment changes to achieve these goals. I was a member of a small group (EnviroTech)[1] formed within a few years of my fieldwork period. The group had been created to focus on potential environmental issues associated with future manufacturing processes. The intern role was a natural one from which to conduct participant observation as I was an accepted, yet temporary, member of the organization and others expected me to observe, question, and learn about their practices. As a participant, and not merely an observer, I had unique access to the member experience. I, too, had to develop work plans, participate in projects, and deliver results and these demands and activities exposed me to cultural norms and practices that might have been less accessible to an observer.

As part of my participant role, I first developed case studies on a number of successful and unsuccessful projects that had been initiated before my arrival or were ongoing. In researching the case studies and other projects, I conducted several dozen semi-structured interviews over the course of my observation period. Typically these interviews probed who was involved, the project history, key challenges, how these were resolved, and interviewee's attributions of factors (for example organizational , technical, and so on) that contributed to the challenges and their resolution. Frequently interviewees provided documents that captured project developments. The interviews and documents were critical data on those projects initiated prior to my participant observation period, with the documents ensuring that I did rely on interviewee's retrospective accounts alone (Golden, 1992). I also used interviews and documents to better understand the projects I was observing. I sought to interview managers and engineers involved in projects from a variety of groups, enabling me to gather information on how the same project was viewed from the perspective of different functional groups and/or different geographical sites.

Following the first three months, once I had largely completed the case studies, I became increasingly involved in several other projects. These projects included helping to prepare an environmental long-range strategic plan for Chipco, developing an environmental module for a materials risk assessment tool, and investigating the possible use of computational modeling of environmental impacts. I attended monthly meetings of the decision-making body for environmental process development (the EnviroCouncil), as well as several industry-wide meetings and followed closely the programs and projects under consideration and development. Over the course of my time in EnviroTech, I took on a number of new projects opportunistically as my manager or I saw a need for someone to represent our group. This helped to expose me to the broadest possible range of the activities of my group, and its interactions with Tech and other groups.

Although my small group was dispersed between three geographical locations in the US, I spent the majority of my time at a single location. I worked in the building occupied by Chipco's Tech (manufacturing process technology development) group. At this site, Chipco's most advanced manufacturing process generation, which would enter the manufacturing fabrication facilities (known as 'fabs') some two years later, was being designed, optimized and evaluated by roughly 1500 engineers and technicians. New process modifications or process equipment that would improve microprocessor performance and speed were all introduced here. New environmental treatment systems were also to be developed and introduced at this location. From this vantage point, I could observe the interface between environmental work and technology development work and also a certain amount of the action on both sides of this interface.

Cultural Analysis

In constructing the description and analysis of the culture of Chipco with a focus on the work on the Tech and environmental groups in Chapters 4 and 5, I drew primarily upon field notes written daily throughout my nine-month participant observation period. I also used interview and documentary data to supplement my field notes, as these sources enabled me to better understand projects and practices that I was observing at the time of the fieldwork as well as gather detail on issues and projects that predated my fieldwork.

Following a grounded theory (Glaser and Strauss, 1967) approach,[2] I read my field notes and interview notes for recurring themes and built up a database consisting of about 1500 observations sorted into about 80 cultural descriptors. Themes emerged around the work itself – how it was organized, what it comprised – as well as more fundamental cultural categories – what was the nature of knowledge, how was time experienced? These cultural themes, and the observations that support them, were used to develop the descriptions of Tech culture in Chapter 4 and contrast it with environmental work in Chapter 5.

Project Analysis

I performed a second analysis that involved an additional coding of the data to understand whether and how the actions taken by those advancing the environmental issues changed over time, and which of these were successful and unsuccessful at influencing Tech. This analysis sorted the data by particular environmental projects undertaken throughout the six year period prior to and during my fieldwork. I looked at seven projects in detail. Each project was aimed at addressing some environmental aspect of a specific manufacturing process under development and each involved interactions between Tech and environmental specialists. Other projects that involved factory-scale changes to address water and energy consumption, or that were focused on the development of strategic plans or models, were not included in this set, so the projects by no means capture all of EnviroTech's activities during this period.

In the six-year period considered, 15 projects that focused on environmental aspects of particular manufacturing processes under development had been initiated, and several interviewees identified the earliest one for which I had data as the first one that had been undertaken. Consistent with the approach of other researchers (Hansen, 1999), I eliminated six projects from the analysis because they were at a very early stage and members were still learning about the environmental issues and initiating action on them. Two further projects were eliminated because I lacked sufficient sources of data on them to triangulate my findings.[3] After eliminating these, I was left with seven projects for analysis, which included both successes and failures.

I performed a detailed within-case analysis (Eisenhardt, 1989; Miles and Huberman, 1994) for each project by assembling all the relevant data for each one and then coding using emergent themes (Glaser and Strauss, 1967; Miles and Huberman, 1994). Because I was looking specifically at how each project proceeded and how those involved sought to overcome challenges to the integration of environmental considerations into manufacturing process development, I coded for moves used by those advancing the issue (what did they say and/or do?), as well as diagnoses (what was wrong?), and evaluations (how successful were any approaches taken?). This project analysis led to an understanding of how environmental problems were set over time, what strategies for action were used to work on them, and how and why these changed over time. Further details on the project analysis are given in Chapter 6.

ENVIRONMENTAL IMPACTS OF SEMICONDUCTOR MANUFACTURING

A semiconductor manufacturer might seem an odd choice for a study of environmental management, for it is not traditionally regarded as a 'dirty' industry. Indeed, the entire US semiconductor industry emits only a tiny fraction – well under one-half of one percent – of the toxic materials released to the environment by the nation's industrial enterprises (EPA, 2003). It consumes a mere one-third of one percent of the energy consumed by US industry (MECS, 2002). In contrast, the chemical manufacturing industry emits 12 percent of the nation's toxic chemical emissions (EPA, 2003) and uses 29 percent of all electricity consumed by US industry (MECS, 2002). The semiconductor industry mobilizes a relatively minute amount of material, most of it silicon dioxide, itself a benign material that is a major component of common beach sand. Coal extraction, an industry with roughly equivalent economic scale to the semiconductor industry in 2002, mobilizes 4.5 billion tons of material annually, while the semiconductor manufacturing industry mobilizes less than 56000 tons of silicon, its primary raw material (Williams, 2003). Water consumption? A similarly small environmental impact relative to other industries is seen. The most recent data available puts water use by the semiconductor industry at one-fifth of one percent, and that by the chemicals industry at 28 percent, of national industrial totals (US Dept. of Commerce, 1986).

Despite the relatively limited absolute scale of its environmental impacts, the semiconductor industry does present significant and specialized environmental challenges associated with its need to maintain a uniquely clean manufacturing environment and the manufacturing process's reliance on small quantities of highly novel organic and inorganic chemicals to achieve desired chip properties. Chip manufacturing is an immensely complex production process, made up of several hundred steps that use chemicals, gases and energies of various forms to pattern, implant and build the layers that make up the finished product. In order to prevent dust particles from destroying the electrical properties of the chip during manufacture, chemical solvents, gases and water are used to keep the silicon wafers on which the chips are created, the process equipment, and the 'fab' (or fabrication facility) in which the manufacturing takes place, scrupulously clean.

All this drives a relatively high use of secondary materials, especially when compared to the minute quantities of materials incorporated into the product. To produce a 2 g chip, only 2 percent (by weight) of which is the silicon 'die,' and 0.2 percent the active circuitry on this die (Murphy *et al.*, 2003), it has been estimated that 1700 g of material is needed (Williams *et al.*, 2002). The great majority of this, 1600 g, is secondary fossil fuel use to provide electricity for manufacturing (Williams *et al.*, 2002); just maintaining the 'clean room' environment in which chips are fabricated consumes as much as 60 percent of the total electrical power used during manufacture (National Academy of Sciences, 1999).

Approximately 72 g of specialty chemicals are used to produce each chip – a factor of about 150 times the final weight of the product (Williams *et al.*, 2002). Despite their relatively small absolute quantities, these chemicals can be of significant concern. One retired manager from a leading chip manufacturer observed that 'the reality of a fabrication plant is that it's a huge chemical factory' (Brumfiel, 2004). The industry uses a number of specialty chemicals that are not used by any other manufacturing industry and the sheer novelty of some of these chemicals is of key concern as little may be known about their potential environmental and health effects. Industry members continue to seek rapid assessment and screening tools that can be used to evaluate chemicals before they are put into the production process (Murphy *et al.*, 2003). Nonetheless, past and continuing attention to the health effects, in particular, of these chemicals suggests that much remains unknown. A 1989 industry-sponsored study led to the elimination of certain solvents following findings on reproductive health effects (Semiconductor Industry Association, 2006a). More recently, the industry announced in 2005 that it retained Vanderbilt University to conduct one of the largest privately sponsored epidemiological studies using retrospective health records from 85 000 workers (Semiconductor Industry Association, 2006a). The effort seeks to assess whether there is an increased cancer risk among chip fabrication workers, compared to other semiconductor industry workers and the general population, as a result of their exposure to chemicals used in fabrication.

Figure 2.1 shows a simplified picture of the major chemical, material, energy and water inputs to and outputs from a typical semiconductor manufacturing process.

It must be noted that considerable environmental benefits have been associated with the electronic products whose production the semiconductor industry supports. Electronics and information technology enable the exchange of information and goods with lower energy and pollution impacts

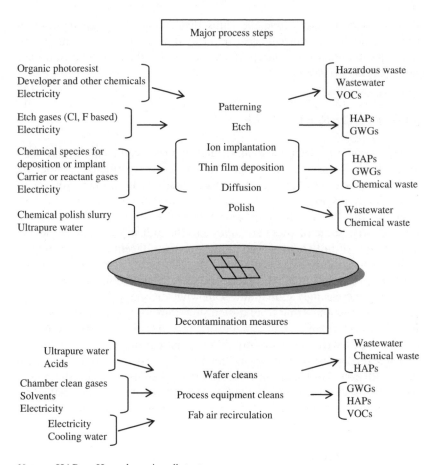

Notes: HAPs = Hazardous air pollutants.
GWGs = Global warming gases.
VOCs = Volatile organic compounds.
Wastewater needs on-site treatment to neutralize acids/bases.
Chemical waste may include hazardous and/or non-hazardous solid waste.

*Figure 2.1   Environmental impacts of major process steps and
decontamination measures in semiconductor manufacturing*

than traditional sectors which rely on material production and transportation (Toffel and Horvath, 2004). Furthermore, electronic controls can be used to make heating, lighting, and production significantly more energy efficient (Horrigan *et al.*, 1998), reducing resource and climate impacts associated with the operation of buildings, equipment and appliances. In recent years, the semiconductor manufacturing industry has not only responded to its customers' requests to make chips that enable power-saving features (for example energy-efficient 'sleep' modes) in products such as laptops and desktop computers, but is also producing chips that themselves consume less power during operation.

THE BIGGER PICTURE

Broader economic, technological, regulatory and social conditions importantly shape the context in which semiconductor manufacturers act on environmental issues. While each company may pay attention to and act on issues differently, in line with the priorities of its culture, there are a number of trends that delimit the scope and nature of environmental practices in this industry. Some of these are unique to the industry – for example, the extreme rate of both historic economic growth and technological change – while others capture more general trends relevant to other manufacturing industries. For example, the semiconductor manufacturing industry is becoming increasingly global and somewhat disaggregated with the separation of manufacturing from design functions for some companies, and the location of many new manufacturing facilities in low-wage developing economies. This trend towards off-shore manufacturing has been occurring for some time in less technologically advanced industries, and will only continue and grow. Understanding the nature of these trends, and the potential issues they present to individual companies, is critical to understanding how external and internal factors interact to influence the environmental actions of a given company.

Economic Conditions

The economic scale of the semiconductor manufacturing industry and its rate of growth is staggering. Worldwide sales of semiconductor products reached a record \$227 billion in 2005; sales from US based semiconductor manufacturers reached \$110 billion in the same year (Semiconductor Industry Association, 2006b). The industry worldwide has sustained a 12 percent annual average growth in sales for the past two decades, with the US-based industry growing slightly faster at an annual average rate of 12.6 percent (Semiconductor Industry Association, 2006b). According to one account it was the 17th largest industry in the US in 1987, and the single largest, measured by its contribution to US gross domestic product, ten years later in 1996 (Pearce, 2005). The semiconductor industry and related high-tech industry account for 30 percent of US economic growth in recent periods (National Academy of Sciences, 1999). The industry is now rapidly growing in other parts of the world. While US manufacturers have historically accounted for between 40 and 50 percent of worldwide sales, and Japanese manufacturers about 40 percent, the Japanese share in particular has eroded since the mid-1990s and sales from manufacturers based in the rest of the world grown from under 20 percent to almost 30 percent in 2005 (Semiconductor Industry Association, 2006b).

Market growth has been fueled by a commensurate growth in manufacturing capacity and output. There are currently approximately 900 chip fabrication plants worldwide (Brumfiel, 2004). Worldwide semiconductor manufacturers increased actual output at an annual average rate of 7.4 percent per year in the decade up to 2005 (Semiconductor Industry Association, 2006c). With this kind of growth, the environmental impacts of semiconductor manufacturing inevitably multiply if the same chemicals and the same environmental control technologies are used, or even if significant improvements are made. For example, while the US semiconductor industry's water consumption per square inch of silicon remained constant for a decade in the 1990s, the number of square inches of silicon processed over the same time period increased by a factor of five, resulting in a five-fold increase in net water demand (Elrod and Worth, 2000). Over a similar period, the industry's chemical use per square inch dropped by almost 30 percent (ibid.), but such a decline did not counteract the contribution from the sheer increase in the quantity of chips produced. The industry's net electricity consumption grew by 27 percent, four times the US industrial average, between 1993 and 1996 (US Dept. of Commerce, 1994, 1996).

While the economic picture for the industry is generally rosy, it is also marked by intense market competition between the major players and characteristic cyclicity, which have their own implications for how environmental demands might be experienced. With the newest, most powerful chips commanding a premium in the market, chip manufacturers compete to improve their manufacturing processes to enable new product introductions every two years or less. This practice drives down prices on older chips, partially contributing to cycles of demand and supply for the industry. These cycles also are driven by orders and inventories in the related computer and electronics industries, and the broader macroeconomic environment. For example, the semiconductor manufacturing industry saw its biggest downturn in sales in 2001, from worldwide sales of $204 billion in 2000 to $139 in 2001 (Semiconductor Industry Association, 2006b). This downturn was attributed to the global recession combined with overcapacity and inventory surpluses that resulted from very rapid growth in the industry in the late 1990s, and a decline in sales of computers and other devices (Pearce, 2005). The nature of competition in the industry, and the erosion of profit margins in recent years as competition only increases, means that environmental improvements, like other operational costs, must often be accompanied by compelling opportunities for productivity improvements and/or cost reductions (Brumfiel, 2004). In this sense, the economic and market environment in which semiconductor manufacturers operate can act as a 'brake' on broad efforts to improve the environmental performance of the industry, an observation that has also been made for the pulp and paper industry (Gunningham *et al.*, 2003).

The sheer cost of research and development to bring about new and improved manufacturing processes and to build fabrication facilities (fabs) to house them also limits potential investment in other areas. In the late 1990s some manufacturers were opening a new fab, at an investment of $1–2 billion per fab, every 9 to 12 months (Resetar, 1999). High costs of production are, as in other industries, driving more and more manufacturing fabs to locate in lower-wage regions of the world. For example, two-thirds of the new state-of-the-art fabs will be built in Asia (Semiconductor Industry Association, 2006d) and many manufacturers now use 'foundries' for at least some of their chip production. Foundries are dedicated contract manufacturers who build chips to others' designs.[4] Not surprisingly, the major foundries are located in countries such as Taiwan where production costs are lower than in the US or Europe. With the division of chip design and production between companies, and the shift in manufacturing to other countries, comes a potential concern about differences in environmental standards and regulatory enforcement between countries. This trend in the globalization of manufacturing is seen in a number of industries and poses new challenges for the monitoring of environmental practice, and determining the standards that should be applied and the nature of their enforcement.

Technological Innovation

Perhaps unique to the semiconductor manufacturing industry and the high-tech sector in general is the continual, high pace of technological innovation. Chipco and other leading chip manufacturers develop a new manufacturing process generation every two years, which involves significantly updating about one-third of the production equipment and modifying, through new chemicals or new process parameters, a number of other aspects of the manufacturing process. Several hundred discrete process steps, typically repeated sequences of eight core operations, are needed to produce a chip. To characterize the associated environmental impacts, evaluate tradeoffs among alternatives (for example if a process step is changed to use more water but less energy, or one chemical is substituted for another, what is the net environmental effect?), and develop equipment or procedures to mitigate the environmental impacts, all within less than a two-year window during the development of a new manufacturing process generation, is a significant technical challenge.

This rapid and sustained change in manufacturing operations brings unique challenges and opportunities for addressing environmental impacts. The opportunity to improve environmental performance by installing new control equipment, or modifying new manufacturing processes using information gained from old ones, presents itself much more frequently than it does in more traditional industries. Compared to the chemical industry where an average manufacturing process may have a lifetime of 15 years and a chemical plant itself a lifetime up to 75 years (Kirschner, 1995), the significant retooling of chip manufacturing fabs every few years creates a window for the installation of new environmental equipment without retrofitting to existing manufacturing equipment. However, the associated challenge is that process development optimizes for process performance, and final selections of chemicals and equipment may not be made until late in the development cycle, leaving little time to understand and address environmental issues. Furthermore, the novelty of some of the chemicals introduced only exaggerates the challenges.

Innovation in this industry also, of course, occurs in the products and their design. New chip designs and features enable new functionality of consumer and business electronics. With more and more electronic devices needing to be portable and instantly accessible, semiconductor manufacturers are responding by designing chips that consume less power, but are durable and take little time to 'power up.' With innovation across the board, and the proliferation of consumer electronics in all forms, the waste produced by 'obsolete' electronic devices – sometimes only a handful of years old – is increasingly becoming a concern. Not only are desktop computers and laptops being produced and replaced at an alarming rate, but so are cell phones, music players and the like; the average cell phone is replaced in the US every 18 months (eBay, 2006). Electronics waste averages 4 percent of the municipal waste stream in European countries, and is growing at three times the rate of other components of the waste stream (Waste Online, 2006). Hazardous materials associated with electronics waste include lead, cadmium, mercury and other heavy metals, flame retardants and various other materials known to be harmful to human health and the environment.

As a result of the growing quantities and the hazards associated with disposal of such waste, the European Union has introduced legislation on waste electronic and electrical equipment (WEEE) requiring that it be recovered from the end consumer for reuse or recycling. A more recent European Union directive (RoHS Directive) restricts the use and quantity of certain chemicals (including lead, cadmium, mercury, hexavalent chromium and certain flame retardants) included in electronics equipment produced in or sold in the EU market. While no such regulatory framework currently exists in the US, several states have proposed or adopted limited electronics waste initiatives, and some nonprofit organizations are developing schemes (such as the Electronic Product Environmental Assessment Tool, EPEAT) to help institutional purchasers identify electronics that meet specified environmental standards. The electronics industry has responded to these trends by initiating some product stewardship efforts, including design and infrastructure to enable collection, disassembly and recycling of products. Most of the major US-based computer manufacturers operate schemes that enable end consumers to return their old computer for donation, auction, or recycling. eBay has entered this area with their 'Rethink' program which connects users with companies, charitable organizations, and each other in order to donate, auction, or recycle computers, cell phones and other electronic devices (eBay, 2006).

This increased attention to electronics waste has been driven back through the supply chain to the semiconductor manufacturers, many of whom now count among their environmental activities the design and stewardship of their products. Again, this trend is a more universal one. Historically the environmental impacts of industry have not been regarded as extending far beyond their fence lines, and pollution has been the major focus of regulatory and public attention. But improvements in the pollution records of virtually all manufacturing industries, coupled with an awareness that some products (for example automobiles) generate far greater environmental impacts during their use and disposal, as opposed to production, has shifted attention to the design of products to minimize their 'lifecycle' environmental impacts. With this trend comes a shift in where environmental considerations enter the company and how they may be represented and worked on.

Pollution has historically been an issue for legal compliance staff, those concerned with factory design and operation, and environmental, health and safety specialists. Product environmental issues may be channeled into the organization through sales, marketing or design teams. They may come from others in the supply chain. For example, many major auto manufacturers now require their suppliers to operate certified environmental management systems to ensure some level of attention to environmental performance of their processes and products. Regardless of their source, the need to respond to such demands, coupled with continued process and product innovation, drive environmental considerations into other aspects of the business, engaging new internal groups in the act of interpreting and acting on such issues.

Regulatory and Non-regulatory Trends

Regulation governing semiconductor manufacturing has changed only slightly over the years, with much more innovation in the area of voluntary programs and negotiated agreements. Voluntary programs can include those initiated by a regulatory agency to recruit corporate participants and encourage them to improve their environmental performance in specific areas by offering some benefit such as technical assistance, increased flexibility in meeting regulatory requirements, and/or recognition. These are typically developed in response to criticisms of the existing regulatory system as inflexible, not encouraging innovation on the part of industry, or achieving its ends at too great a cost to industry. Members of the US semiconductor manufacturing industry have participated in several voluntary efforts developed by the Environmental Protection Agency (EPA). These include the now defunct Common Sense Initiative, launched to engage specific industry sectors in discussions of smarter, cheaper approaches to environmental protection for their sector, and Project XL, which invited proposals for innovative environmental approaches from individual companies and facilities.

Negotiated industry-government agreements are typically used to address a well-defined environmental issue associated with one industry sector, possibly preempting or postponing anticipated regulation by developing a memorandum of understanding (MOU) between government regulators and an individual company or industry sector. The semiconductor manufacturing industry has used this approach to limit the emissions of chemicals with known environmental and/or human health effects, while still retaining the ability to use chemicals that are critical to the production process. In 1996 the US semiconductor industry reached an agreement with the EPA in which it committed to reduce its emissions of a class of high global warming potential (GWP) gases, known collectively as PFCs (perfluorocompounds). Three years later the World Semiconductor Council (WSC), comprised of every major regional semiconductor trade association announced a similar voluntary commitment to reduce PFC emissions by 10 percent by 2010, from a baseline year that differed by region[5] (World Semiconductor Council, 1999). In 2006, the WSC announced a second voluntary agreement among its members to curtail emissions of perfluorooctyl sulfonate (PFOS)-based chemicals, considered persistent organic pollutants (POPs) by a number of countries, and to search for alternative chemicals (Semiconductor Industry Association, 2006e). In each case, the chemicals are considered essential to chip manufacture, and the quantity used was expected to increase with the increasing complexity of the manufacturing process over time. A negotiated agreement is therefore a way for industry members to ensure that they continue to have access to critical process chemicals, but also to put measures in place to reduce use and emissions and accelerate the development of alternatives. The threat of regulation is always present, giving the regulatory agency some degree of power in enforcing the terms of the agreement.

Negotiated and voluntary approaches are gaining ground across a number of industries as governments and companies themselves look for new ways to address increasingly complex environmental challenges without imposing costly, inefficient 'one-size-fits-all' technological or operational standards. In particular, members of industries are increasingly developing voluntary standards or codes to guide the practices of their members, or are signing on to government-sponsored programs designed to achieve similar ends (Coglianese and Nash, 2002). Some of the industry-led programs are now certified by third parties, ensuring that member companies have put in place particular management practices, specific environmental goals, and measures to meet them. While these types of approaches undoubtedly give companies more discretion and control over how they meet certain environmental objectives, they can also be criticized, by outsiders and participants alike, for not establishing clear and consistent targets for environmental performance. As the Clean Air project at Chipco demonstrates, external standards (for example the emissions threshold below which Chipco could make process changes more easily) are sometimes important motivators for internal action. For this reason, the emergence and development of a range of voluntary programs, negotiated agreements, and other types of policy instruments deserves close attention for how they influence actions within a range of industries and individual companies. Research already shows that the intended benefits of some of these programs do not match participants' perceptions of the benefits because these perceptions are informed by factors internal to the firm which can differ widely even between firms facing similar external pressures (Howard-Grenville *et al.*, 2006).

Social Pressures

Unlike a number of more traditional manufacturing sectors (for example chemicals, mining and oil and gas industries), the semiconductor manufacturing industry has not attracted sustained, national or international attention to its environmental practices by activist groups. Perhaps because it is perceived as a 'clean' industry, or because the quantity of material it mobilizes is far outreached by the more traditional industries, community and broader social concern over the industry's environmental record has been relatively limited and quite localized. Activist and community groups have mobilized to protest the siting and development of several US semi-conductor fabrication facilities, largely over concerns about a fab's demand on limited regional water resources, or more general concerns about toxic chemical use and potential risks to the adjacent community. Some of these groups have focused on the industry more broadly, calling for attention to fab energy consumption, labor practices, and worker health.[6] The industry as a whole has similarly experienced relatively limited shareholder activism, with some shareholder resolutions brought by investment firms to individual companies, typically requesting greater disclosure of environmental practices and performance, or calling for commitments to improve specific aspects of environmental performance.

The industry garners at least as much positive attention for its social record as it does negative. Many of the leading companies are ranked highly on key indices of corporate responsibility, including the Dow Jones Sustainability Index, the Global 100 established by the World Economic Forum, and by socially responsible investment firms such as Calvert. These indices attempt to capture factors that may make companies more effective than their peers at managing the opportunities and costs associated with the company's impact on the environment and the communities in which it operates, as well as its workplace practices (for example labor relations, diversity), governance and business practices. Consistent with increasing attention to corporate responsibility across a wide range of companies, many members of the electronics and computer industries now publish broad corporate responsibility reports. Of the electronics industry companies that are among the world's 250 largest companies, 91 percent publish such reports (KPMG, 2005).

The shift in attention from strictly environmental impacts to environmental and social impacts of the industry is again consistent with broader trends influencing the practices of companies across industries, particularly manufacturers and multinationals. It represents a widening of the nature of demand that are brought to companies and an expansion of the channels through which they are brought. Despite considerable differences in how environmental and other social issues are measured and monitored, they are increasingly being brought together, not just in corporate responsibility reports, but also in the demands brought by advocacy groups, and in management functions within companies. As this continues, the complexities of addressing environmental issues may only increase. On the other hand, sustained attention to corporate responsibility may bring environmental and social issues under the same banner within a dedicated functional group in some companies, to the detriment of efforts to actually integrate environmental issues into the day-to-day work of those who can most directly influence it. Indeed, the type of response a company takes will likely depend on how it perceives the opportunities or threats associated with demands for corporate responsibility, which, like environmental demands alone, are interpreted through existing cultural categories and meanings.

Summing Up the Bigger Picture

In sum, the external conditions and trends that the semiconductor manufacturing industry is subject to are rich and complex. The nature of market competition, the rate of growth, pace of technological change (in both processes and products), shift in regulatory approaches, and emerging shift in attention to broader social impacts of the industry's activities all produce conditions that strongly influence what goes on within individual companies in this industry. While some of these are specific to the industry, they are by no means fully unique. Every manufacturing industry today faces technological change (albeit, at different paces), shifts in the nature of competition due to globalization and other macroeconomic trends, and changing social demands along with altered regulatory approaches in many jurisdictions. The in-depth analysis of Chipco brings into focus how these factors are interpreted and acted upon in one particular setting, and serves as a microcosm in which to develop greater insight into how these trends may play out more generally in other companies and industries.

NOTES

1. EnviroTech, Tech, and other group and individual names used in this book, are pseudonyms.
2. Grounded theory is an approach used to discover theory from data, rather than to disprove a priori hypotheses using data. In a grounded theory approach, coding of data and its analysis are performed jointly, with new data being constantly compared to earlier data to generate plausible categories and hypotheses (Glaser and Strauss, 1967).
3. For the first project I had only two interviews and could not obtain enough other interviews and archival documents to corroborate the information obtained in the interviews. For the second, I had only a few documents and limited observational data, and no interviews. As all the other projects I analyzed in depth had a combination of comprehensive interview, archival, and observational data, and typically all three, I felt any analysis of these two projects would not be comparable.
4. This business model separates out the design and layout of chips, itself an intensive and highly competitive activity, from their actual production. Several semiconductor companies today are completely 'fabless,' meaning that they design chips and rely entirely on foundries for their production.
5. This baseline year is 1995 for the US.
6. For example, the Silicon Valley Toxics Coalition has been active in this area for a number of years and counts among its activities advancing environmental sustainability and clean production, expressing concern for environmental and social justice, and seeking democratic decision-making for communities and workers affected by the high-tech revolution in Silicon Valley and elsewhere.

3. Nature and culture

Any given environment we know ... exists as a structure of meaningful distinctions.

(Douglas, 1972: 139)

Members of any culture, including organizational cultures, hold particular and partial views of the natural environment and appropriate actions toward it. Broad trends, such as those outlined in the previous chapter, can capture and bound the scope and character of a company's interactions with the environment, but the details of such interactions also depend on how the company's members perceive the issues, label them as problems, and set about fixing them. A company's culture can be a central force in shaping how its managers and employees select issues for attention, and how they act on such issues. As a result, a company's actions 'out there' in the environment cannot be fully divorced from what goes on inside, in the dynamic workings of its culture.

In this chapter, I lay the groundwork for the description and analysis of Chipco's culture and its influence on the company's environmental actions that is explored in the next three chapters. To do this, I first argue that ideas of what constitutes the natural environment, how one should feel about it, and how one should act in relation to it have always said at least as much about human cultures as they have said about the biophysical environment. 'Nature' and 'environment' reference not just some physical inventory, but carry significant cultural and historical meaning. I then outline an evolution in the demands for corporate environmental practice over the last few decades to capture the different, and increasingly complex ways in which environmental issues have shown up for companies.

Prominent academic explanations have recognized this evolution and have sought to account for new and diverse drivers of corporate environmental practices. I review two key theoretical approaches, one rooted in economic theory, and one rooted in sociology. There are recent moves to articulate differences that might refine our understanding of how individual companies make sense of complex demands and opportunities for addressing environmental issues. Internal factors have attracted relatively little attention, however. In the final section of the chapter I bring in theory on organizational culture and use it to explain why understanding culture can shed light on a company's environmental actions.

It does little good, however, to argue that 'culture matters' without specifying how it matters. Organizational cultures do not fatalistically determine action within companies, nor are they uniformly shared. In the latter part of the chapter I explore the implications of the existence of different subcultures, and differences in power between such groups. In this case, whose interpretations of issues will matter? Which cultural categories will be invoked? What kinds of actions will be taken? And, critically, how can those who are trying to introduce new concerns make their voices heard? I connect to the work on 'issue selling' as a form of influence behavior undertaken by those who typically are unable to set the agenda for what constitutes an important issue within an organization. When one group's culture is dominant, others may have to work to tap into their concerns by skillfully selling their issues. This opens up a way of seeing a company's culture and the distinctions it draws not simply as a constraint on action toward the environment, but also as a vehicle for gradual, bottom-up change.

WHAT IS NATURE?

Why is nature such contested ground? Can we pin down what it means? Not likely. Ideas of the environment and nature have always been many and diverse. 'Nature' and 'environment' are used at times to draw attention to what they exclude: the technological artifacts created by human action – cities, cars, electric toothbrushes – and the non-physical but nonetheless tangible outputs of human endeavor – laws, ceremonies, and poetry. At other times, these words are used to refer to things with physical existence and generative forces of their own – cyclones, mountains and tadpoles. Perhaps more important than the things they name (or don't name) is what these labels say about such things. Nature is at times fearsome, powerful, chaotic and outside the realm of human control; at other times it is pure, unspoiled, balanced, and a garden for retreat from human civilization. It is subject to scientific study to reveal its underlying 'law,' yet also admired for a beauty that cannot be reproduced by human means. The environment has value because of what it gives – water, medicinals, shelter – and what it cannot give – open space, untrammeled wilderness.

For every environmentalist, like Bill McKibben, who mourns that man's manipulation of his environment has ushered in the 'end of nature' – that 'separate and wild province, the world apart from man to which he adapted, under whose rules he was born and died,' (1990: 43) – there is a technological optimist, like Jesse Ausubel, who celebrates man's 'liberation' from the environment and sees a coming 'highly efficient hydrogen economy, landless agriculture, industrial ecosystems in which waste virtually disappears' as evidence that 'science and technology are ready . . . to reconcile our economy and the environment' (1996: 15).

For every believer in the balance of nature who is concerned that human activity does not force nature too far from its own, self-correcting course, there is a close observer of history, who reminds us that 'the conviction that nature is a stable, holistic, homeostatic community capable of preserving its natural balance more or less indefinitely if only humans can avoid "disturbing" it . . . is in fact a deeply problematic assumption' (Cronon, 1996: 24).

Perhaps the only commonality across all these views is the observation that nature is contested terrain and inevitably so. Environmental historian William Cronon suggests that 'because people differ in their beliefs, because their visions of the true, the good, and the beautiful are not always the same, they inevitably differ as well in their understanding of what nature means and how it should be used – because nature is so often the place where we go searching for the fulfillment of our desires' (1996: 51). My nature and your nature may be quite different, even though we breath the same air and tread the same ground.

Contested conceptions of nature and the environment are not new. Throughout literary and political history differing ideas of nature have been invoked to support seemingly disparate projects. Historian Raymond Williams suggests that 'the idea of nature contains, though often unnoticed, an extraordinary amount of human history' (1980: 67). Where in Hobbes' 'state of nature' men would be engaged in an incessant struggle for power and life would be 'solitary, poore, nasty, brutish, and short' (1651: 186) without the order imposed by a monarch, Locke's state of nature was a peaceable community in which men would attend to the 'preservation of the life, the liberty, health, limb, or goods of another' (1690: 120).

The only constant in these examples is that the natural and the cultural often stand in some sort of dialectical relationship: the natural as model for human civilization, or as a state preceding the civilizing effects of human society; the natural as embodying perfection unattainable by man, or as a template for the application of man's unique capacity for reason. As anthropologist Mary Douglas argues, 'it is only by exaggerating the difference between within and without, . . . that a semblance of order is created' (1966: 7). And once there is order, there can be action. If nature is ideal or wild, benevolent or efficient, the prescription for human interaction with it follows – copy it, tame it, worship it, cultivate it, study it, . . . the list goes on.

NATURE AND THE CORPORATION

How does this diversity of ideas about nature and the environment show up in the actions taken by the modern corporation, and in explanations offered for such actions? By and large, it doesn't, and it hasn't. Others have pointed out that early literature on corporate environmental management largely accepted a fairly unitary view of the environment, often portraying as relatively simple and unidirectional the relationship between social forces, law, and corporate environmental practices (Coglianese, 2001). Indeed, the early history of corporate environmental management suggests that environmental issues and the actions needed to address them *were* relatively clear and well defined for corporations. But, as this section outlines, the issues and actions became much more complex and multifaceted over time. Companies now experience environmental issues in a dramatically different way than they did when industrial pollution was first regulated more than three decades ago. After tracing some of the factors that contributed to this evolution, I then address how prominent explanations for corporate environmental management have attempted to keep pace.

Trends in Environmental Management Demands and Practice

Regulation was the primary driver of environmental management activity by firms beginning in the 1970s. The first significant regulatory requirements for pollution control entered force in the US in the early 1970s and defined as environmental ills the industrial pollution of the nation's air, land and waterways. The US experience was not atypical, with most nations assuming considerably greater responsibility for the state of the environment, primarily through the use of industrial environmental regulation, after 1970 (Frank *et al.*, 2000). Relative to what came later, with the advent of new forms of regulation, new levels of public disclosure and new environmental concerns, this was a period during which environmental issues for industry were well defined and more or less consistent. The primary regulatory approach adopted in the US was labeled 'command-and-control' because it established detailed requirements for how firms had to comply with specific standards, often by delineating minimum acceptable control technologies and/or maximum allowable emissions levels. Such a regulatory approach, also adopted internationally, served to make the actions expected of industry relatively unambiguous. Social pressures were regarded as largely subsumed in regulation, as social concern expressed in the 1960s and the early 1970s over industrial pollution and environmental degradation was seen to shape federal, state, and local regulatory responses in the 1970s and the early 1980s (Hoffman, 1999; Coglianese, 2001). Finally, during this time, a firm's obligation to meet regulatory requirements was typically seen as a trade-off with economic concerns. Environmental management was regarded as costly, not as a source of competitive advantage or cost savings.

From regulatory compliance to social obligations and economic opportunities

Only in the mid- to late- 1980s did a number of companies begin to experience demands for environmental practice as coming from numerous and new sources, including social and economic spheres. High-profile disasters like the release of a toxic chemical cloud from a Union Carbide plant in Bhopal, India, along with growing public concern about the safety and siting of industrial plants, helped to shift attention to issues of transparency and community protection. Agenda 21, the document prepared by the 1992 United Nations Conference on Environment and Development (UNCED), known as the 'Earth Summit,' called for countries to establish chemical emissions inventories and make them publicly available. While such attention and efforts would eventually usher in new legislation requiring public disclosure of chemical emissions by facilities in a number of industrialized countries, the US Toxic Release Inventory (TRI), established in 1986, was the first of its kind. It requires that individual industrial facilities collect and report data on releases to the environment (air, land or water), and transfers (to waste or recycling), of a large number of toxic chemicals (currently 650). Such mandatory requirements for chemical reporting were implemented (largely in the late 1990s) in a number of European countries, as well as Canada, Australia, and Japan. Less developed economies, such as Mexico, followed suit much later.

While the establishment of these 'right-to-know' laws added new complexity to the environmental regulation faced by companies, it also brought public perception to bear on what constituted an environmental ill, and companies became increasingly beholden to satisfying the demands and expectations of the public. With the spread of internet access and technology, individuals could now easily obtain the names of polluters in their communities, the type and quantities of chemicals they emit, and track these trends over time. The very act of summarizing and publicly reporting total chemical releases also served as a 'wake-up' call for many managers in US companies and facilities. In 1987, Monsanto CEO Richard Mahoney responded to his company's TRI numbers with a vow to reduce emissions by 90 percent over five years (Mahoney, 1996), pushing other companies to follow suit in TRI emissions reduction efforts. Even those less progressive at least sought to avoid a place on *Fortune* magazine's list of laggards on environmental issues.[1]

Of course, social pressures for improved corporate environmental practice in the 1980s came from many other sources, as attention to local as well as regional (acid rain) and global (ozone depletion) problems continued or emerged, triggered by scientific discovery, actions of nongovernmental organizations, and media attention. Certain dramatic events attracted significant media and public attention, like the 1989 spill of 11 million gallons of crude oil from the *Exxon Valdez* off the coast of Alaska. Exxon's mishandling of communications and refusal to take responsibility in the aftermath of this event served as emblematic of corporate arrogance toward the environment for many environmental activists and members of the general public. The record punitive damages – $5 billion – handed out by the jury in this case reflected solid, and perhaps growing, social concern about company's impacts on the environment, or at least those that were closely documented and watched by the world. Company managers saw the potential for their reputation to plummet overnight, as Exxon's had, as the result of poor environmental practices.

Environmental issues also began to be more clearly and positively connected with economic considerations by company managers in the mid-1980s. Where compliance with regulation had been regarded as a necessary cost of doing business for most companies, a new emphasis on the financial benefits of reducing pollution emerged during this period. In the US, a few companies including 3M and Dow Chemical led the charge and found that avoiding the production of pollution through process changes, material changes, and improved process control not only reduce emissions but saved considerable sums of money. For example, 3M started its Pollution Prevention Pays (3P) program in 1975 and calculated the company avoided 1 billion pounds of pollutant emissions between 1975 and 1992, and saved over $500 million in costs as a result. Advocates of pollution prevention highlighted economic and environmental 'win-win' outcomes, and some argued that pollution prevention and waste minimization would become a key source of competitive advantage for companies who could see and seize the opportunities (Porter and van der Linde, 1995). Pollution prevention, or 'source reduction' as it is sometimes called, is now practiced in industrialized countries around the world, with numerous government programs set up to provide technical support for companies, exchange of best practices, and in some cases, grant support for process improvements. Networks or roundtables of pollution prevention programs now operate as sources of information and exchange about such activities around the globe.

Pollution prevention and toxics release reporting were both trends that, while signaling new ways of thinking about companies' environmental impacts, responsibilities, and opportunities, were largely internally focused. That is, a company embracing these approaches would measure and deeply understand its emission sources, alter and optimize production processes or materials to reduce them, and perhaps develop new technologies or capabilities internally to enable this. Such activities demanded little work beyond the boundaries of the facility, as waste minimization and production efficiency were largely operational, and to a lesser degree, behavioral concerns within a plant. Furthermore, the focus of such activities was to redress inefficiencies of the past, altering or incrementally improving existing production processes without radically changing production approaches, product design, or actual products. What came next forced a much more pluralistic and cross-cutting approach to environmental management, as over the next decade and a half the nature of environmental issues further evolved, as did the nature of the demands, and the need for fundamentally new approaches including attention to design, partnerships between companies, their suppliers, regulators, and even competitors and NGOs.

More complex issues, more diverse approaches

In the mid-1990s, the environmental issues companies faced and the actions they took shifted again, with repercussions that continue to this day. Companies began to grapple with potential solutions for complex, global problems like climate change and persistent, bioaccumulative chemicals, and in a more sophisticated way with local and regional issues like ecosystem disruption, water consumption, and even the impacts of employee commuting. Such issues not only expanded the scope of environmental impacts individual companies were considered responsible for, but also shifted attention to how companies could, collectively, address problems that were global in scale and to which each individual entity contributed some (unequal) fraction of the total.

Global climate change is the ultimate example of such an issue and is gaining attention from companies across a wide spectrum of industries, from energy producers, to major energy consumers, to manufacturers of consumer products that consume large amounts of energy over their lifetimes. The list does not end here, with insurers, investors and funders also altering the way they do business based on the risk associated with their client's greenhouse gas emissions. New regulatory approaches are being adopted for curbing and stabilizing greenhouse gas emissions (largely carbon dioxide, but also methane, nitrous oxides, and some fluorinated compounds). Many of these include market mechanisms designed to cost effectively and collectively reduce greenhouse gas emissions across companies and even across nations. The largest such scheme is the European Union's Emissions Trading Scheme (EU-ETS) which opened in January 2005 and covers electricity generators and members of six major industries in 25 European states. Facilities buy and sell emissions 'allowances' on a market, with those who are able to reduce emissions intendedly benefiting from the sale of allowances to others who cannot make sufficient reductions economically. Even in the United States, one of two countries that did not sign the Kyoto Protocol establishing targets for emissions reductions, an evolving 'patchwork quilt' of local, state, and regional schemes to encourage reductions is taking shape (Hoffman, 2006).

While some of the elements of coping with climate change resemble traditional approaches to environmental management – creating and tracking emissions inventories, setting reductions targets, implementing process improvements – the scope and scale of the issue also demands new approaches. Scenario planning, adaptation of business approaches (particularly those that involve physical assets threatened or already subject to change by climate alterations), and the pursuit of new business opportunities are all on the agendas of leading companies addressing this issue (Hoffman, 2006).

Climate change is but one of the new issues gaining companies' attention. Throughout the latter part of the 1990s and into the 2000s attention to other environmental issues had continued to evolve, with more diverse demands being made and more varied approaches adopted. New social demands were brought. For example, the environmental justice movement gained prominence as it sought to redress the unequal distribution of environmental ills among communities. Its voice became increasingly important in the siting and development of new industrial facilities, or in regional and local issues that cut across industries, such as water consumption. Nontraditional alliances formed around newly emerging issues, including one that sprang up between environmentalists, religious groups, consumer health advocates, scientists and agricultural interests opposed to genetic modification.

New approaches to process and product development were pursued, with some companies shifting their attention from the environmental impacts of production to the 'lifecycle' environmental impacts of products in use and through disposal (Ehrenfeld, 1997; Graedel, 1997). 'Product stewardship' became a new goal for many companies as they responded to either consumer demand, emerging legislation, or simply opportunities to reduce costs through refurbishing and remanufacturing rather than building products from virgin materials. Xerox estimates its comprehensive approach to remanufacturing its copier machines, and reusing parts from copiers and printers, has diverted close to 150 million pounds of material annually that would otherwise have gone to landfill. In some countries and regions, product stewardship has become mandated with laws requiring producers to either take back or ensure the recycling or correct disposal of their goods.

Such approaches are particularly prominent in the auto and electronics industries, and more established in Europe than in the United States.

Other regulatory and voluntary approaches also emerged during this time, many of them coming from government-industry negotiated agreements, or from coordinated industry actions. Following the lead of chemical industry associations in Canada and the US who had developed Responsible Care® codes of environment, health and safety practice for their members in the mid-1980s, a number of industries generated their own voluntary codes for environmental practice (Howard *et al.*, 2000). Regulatory agencies, especially those at the federal and state level in the US experimented with new forms of negotiated agreements and regulatory incentive programs (Coglianese and Nash, 2002) in an effort to induce superior environmental performance from companies at lower cost.

With the natural environment itself now represented as a complex constellation of regulatory limits, public demands, voluntary industry commitments, and economic opportunities, prescriptions for action by companies had become similarly more complex. The ongoing evolution of environmental science only added to a sense of uncertainty and shifting responsibilities around such issues. Compliance with regulation perhaps had once been enough; indeed, in 1970 economist Milton Friedman argued that any further actions beyond compliance constituted 'pure and unadulterated socialism' (1970: 33). But by the late 1990s and early 2000s, 'beyond compliance' initiatives were undertaken with increasing frequency by companies, and explanations for them increasingly sought by scholars. What is the relationship between nature and the corporation, according to contemporary business scholarship? Which aspects of interactions between company decisions, actions and the natural world does such work focus on? And on which aspects does it remain silent?

SCHOLARLY APPROACHES TO NATURE AND THE CORPORATION

Many efforts have been made through business and management scholarship to understand relationships between companies and the environment. In the past ten years, every major management journal has published articles on business and the environment, with the majority of these addressing environmental outcomes (62 percent) as opposed to simply organizational outcomes (19 percent) or treating environmental issues as the context for exploring other organizational phenomena (15 percent) (Bansal and Gao, 2006). Within this relatively robust field of inquiry, most articles use theories grounded in the economic, strategic tradition, with fewer building on sociological theories, and fewer still on psychological theories (Bansal and Gao, 2006). Without attempting a comprehensive review, I briefly consider here two prominent explanations for corporate environmental practice, the strategic argument that 'it pays to be green,' and the institutional argument that 'the rules of the game are shifting.' Following this, I focus on how factors internal to companies, including culture, might open up new ways of explaining firm behavior on environmental issues.

'It Pays to be Green'

The logic of the 'it pays to be green' argument is founded on the observation that pollution, and waste in general, represents for firms 'unproductive resource utilization' (Porter and Van der Linde, 1995: 107). Sound competitive strategy would suggest that companies that reduce their waste production will simultaneously improve environmental performance, reduce costs and, through this, improve their competitiveness. Indeed, Porter and Van der Linde (1995) argued that more stringent regulation benefits firms because it encourages technological innovation, the fruits of which offset the costs of regulatory compliance. If it really does pay to be green, we would expect a correlation between companies' environmental performance and their financial performance, but such a relationship is tenuous. Jaffe and others found, based on a comprehensive survey of the literature, 'little or no evidence supporting the . . . hypothesis that environmental regulation stimulates innovation and improved international competitiveness,' (Jaffe *et al.*, 1995: 159). Russo and Fouts (1997) showed a positive correlation between corporate environmental performance and profitability, moderated by industry growth, but also pointed to a number of earlier studies which reached opposing or indefinite conclusions. No clearer answer is given by a recent extensive meta-analysis of the literature on corporate social performance (Margolis and Walsh, 2003); here a positive association is found in most of the 127 studies that have tried to relate company's social performance to their financial performance, but the validity and reliability of such studies continues to be questioned because of difficulties in establishing meaningful measurements and controls.

There are several ways in which scholars have expanded on the simple question of whether environmental performance – particularly that which goes beyond compliance – is related to near-term financial performance. First, some have dropped the requirement that environmental activities and approaches must show up directly in near-term financial performance, suggesting instead that a company's environmental approaches may comprise a distinct capability that sets it apart from competitors in the marketplace, or among other stakeholders (Sharma and Vredenburg, 1998) and that less tangible benefits (for example brand loyalty) may be the result. This builds on the resource-based view from the strategy literature that posits that companies with valuable, rare, and hard to imitate resources will experience sustained competitive advantage (Wernerfelt, 1984; Barney, 1991). Resources have been viewed fairly broadly, to include physical, human and organizational assets that are strategically relevant (Barney, 1991) and even to include a company's culture that might enable it to envision or portray a valued position in the market (Barney, 1986). Others have added that the ability to combine resources in valuable ways, and the capacity to learn from and adapt to the external environment are important to producing valued firm outcomes such as cost savings and safety performance (Christmann, 2000; Marcus and Nichols, 1999).

The *natural* resource based view builds on this to argue that companies possessing the resources and capabilities to act in accordance with the biophysical constraints posed by earth's natural systems will be more successful in the long run (Gladwin *et al.*, 1995; Hart, 1995). This argument flows from the observation that as natural resources, the source of all manufacturing activity, are further depleted, and/or natural 'sinks' which absorb the waste produced by manufacturing activity, become full, the planet's biophysical capacity becomes an economic (and material) constraint for firms. Hart asserts that 'one of the most important drivers of new resource and capability development for firms will be the constraints and challenges posed by the natural (biophysical) environment' (1995: 989). Those who are able to see the significance of this and build appropriate capabilities will be ahead of their competitors as the external conditions change.

But time horizon is important for this argument as well. Where the simple 'pays to be green' assertion takes too near-term and restricted a view, the natural resource based view may assume too long-term and open a view for many of today's companies. Only a small fraction of firms, like outdoor-gear manufacturer Patagonia, are distinguished by a deep integration of concern for environmental impact into everything they do. The observable environmental actions of the majority of others, however, do not signal that biophysical constraints are perceived as imposing significant immediate or anticipated economic or other costs. For example, it still pays handsomely to be engaged in oil exploration, extraction, refining and distribution, despite the fact that oil is a finite, non-renewable resource whose use has significant environmental impacts. Concern about climate change has compelled many major oil companies now to invest heavily in developing alternative energy technologies, but none have metaphorically 'jumped ship.' Instead, they are hedging against a carbon-constrained future by incrementally diversifying their strategies rather than rapidly (or even gradually) switching their strategic direction.

This relates to the second way scholars are deepening their questions around environmental practices and firm outcomes. If it always 'pays' in some way to be greener than competitors, why don't we see an incessant race to the top in environmental approaches? Here many have noted that firms face neither identical constraints and opportunities in their external environments, nor do they operate with the same internal approaches, suggesting that what is beneficial to one firm may not be so across the board. Indeed, recent work on competitive environmental strategy has shifted to focus less on the question of whether it pays to be green, but when and how it may pay (Reinhardt, 1999; Aragon-Correa and Sharma, 2003). Under certain economic and competitive conditions, but not others, a firm may differentiate itself in the marketplace by virtue of its environmental activities and customers may be willing to pay a premium (Reinhardt, 1999); under certain conditions, but not others, environmental practices yield competitive advantages for firms (Esty and Porter 1998). The uncertainty and complexity of the general business environment, and manager's perceptions of this uncertainty or complexity, can also influence whether proactive environmental strategies will be beneficial or not for firms (Aragon-Correa and Sharma, 2003). This has led to a contingency approach to the natural resource based view (Aragon-Correa and Sharma, 2003), essentially arguing that firms will, or ought to, develop internal resources – such as specific environmental approaches – that fit the external conditions they face.

By moving toward greater concern for managerial perceptions and internal capabilities, the natural resource based view has moved considerably beyond simplistic assertions that 'it pays to be green.' But the approach remains somewhat prescriptive, in assuming that companies will develop internal resources that enable them to improve some performance outcome. Unlike the literature on organizational culture and sociological approaches in general, the strategy literature does not allow for the possibility that internal managerial approaches might 'take on a life of their own' shaping actions on environment and other issues in ways that might not directly connect to performance outcomes, or that do connect but by a path that is more circuitous and less obvious than outside observers would expect.

'The Rules of the Game are Shifting'

A second key explanation for corporate environmental practices has centered on sociological, as opposed to economic or strategic, arguments. The logic here is that companies act within a set of norms that are collectively established, and altered, by many organizational and individual actors, including regulators, the legal system, activists, communities and the public at large. These institutional norms – 'rules of the game' – define what are acceptable, legitimate, and valued behaviors for companies operating in a given historical, social and regulatory climate. Institutions have been defined as 'cognitive, normative, and regulative structures and activities that provide stability and meaning to social behavior' (Scott, 1995), but recent work has moved away from an emphasis on the stability of norms and toward an emphasis on the cognitive and political processes by which collective norms emerge, shape and are shaped by organizational and individual actors (DiMaggio, 1991; Hoffman, 1999; Greenwood *et al.*, 2002; Maguire *et al.*, 2004).

Where companies were once seen as more or less 'passive recipients' (Fligstein, 2001: 110) of norms surrounding business practice, they are now seen as importantly contributing to these norms. In other words, on this view, norms for environmental practice are influenced, but not entirely determined by, members of companies and industries themselves. Trade associations, competitors and professionals within companies can establish and operate to certain norms that reflect their collective experiences and needs.

The institutional perspective differs from a strategic one in which individual companies act in their own best interests in the face of external conditions. To institutionalists, companies' actions – and all of economic activity – are 'embedded' in social structures that constrain some actions but enable others through the operation of norms of trust and reciprocity that derive from social interaction (Dacin *et al.*, 1999; Smith-Doerr and Powell, 2005). A company may be embedded in one or many 'organizational fields' – communities of organizations whose members interact with each other and share common norms or rules (Scott, 1995). Where these fields were once seen as homogeneous and relatively stable, they are now seen as arenas of contestation and debate (Hoffman, 1999; Creed *et al.*, 2002) where norms are continually evolving. What comprised acceptable environmental practice in the past is no longer acceptable today. What comprises acceptable environmental practice today will almost certainly be unacceptable in the future. Institutional arguments seek to explain such evolutions, with a focus on changes in the membership of fields, and the dominant practices and 'rules of the game' within them.

For example, in his comprehensive historical examination of environmentalism and the US chemical and petroleum industries, Hoffman shows how the members of the organizational field changed, as did the meaning of environmentalism that was collectively constructed by these members (1999, 2001). In the 1970s corporate environmental practices were largely responses to regulatory requirements; companies put their efforts into complying with legislation and resisting additional regulation. But a series of disruptive events – including changes in EPA administration, major accidents and spills, and new discoveries about the state of the environment – heralded change in two subsequent periods. From 1983–8, Hoffman argues, environmentalism became more normative for the chemical industry; companies saw environmental management as socially responsible and started to cooperate with the EPA. From 1989–93, environmentalism was starting to become more deeply embedded in the meaning of what it is to be a chemical company; companies focused on management solutions and on merging economic and environmental concerns (Hoffman, 1999).

While institutional perspectives can, over a long period of time and across a large number of organizations, identify and explain the emergence of patterns of norms and behavior, they do not predict future patterns, nor can they easily account for individual company differences in environmental practices. Companies are capable of resisting, countering or strategically adopting practices that are more broadly shared (Powell and DiMaggio, 1991; Oliver, 1991; Fligstein, 1997), and it is difficult to understand motivations for these approaches without understanding more about the individual companies themselves.

Indeed, both the institutional and strategic perspectives on corporate environmental management may be better suited to explaining broader trends than they are to explaining individual differences. A recent book that examined regulatory, social and economic conditions shaping companies' tacit 'licenses to operate' within a single industry reflects this concern (Gunningham *et al.*, 2003). The authors identify some broad trends but conclude that we 'still know little about why individual corporations behave the way they do in the environmental context, about why some companies, but not others, choose to move beyond compliance, or what motivates them to do so' (Gunningham *et al.*, 2003: 135). This internal motivational puzzle is addressed next.

Peering In . . .

While pressures for corporate environmental practice once were, perhaps, relatively unambiguous and unidirectional, the previous section argued that they have become much more complex and interdependent. As a result, manager's perceptions of the issues, their sense of the scope and nature of their company's responsibilities, and their expectations about the trajectory of environmental issues and external pressures should matter now more than ever in explaining firms' environmental actions. Scholarship on corporate environmental management has gradually caught up with these developments. Where early work on the 'greening of industry' advanced the idea that companies evolve through stages (Hunt and Auster, 1990; Roome,

1992) as they adopt increasingly enlightened environmental practices in response to demands from regulators, customers and financial markets (Gladwin *et al.*, 1995; Shrivastava, 1995), recent work demonstrates that individual companies pursue different paths, even when they face seemingly similar external pressures (Prakash, 2000; Gunningham *et al.*, 2003).

If the external pressures on firms – be they economic, social, regulatory, or, more likely, some combination of these – are inadequate to explain their environmental actions, there remains only one other obvious place to look: inside. More scholars are turning their attention to the internal factors that might be shaping choices made about corporate environmental practice. Some point out that managers, not 'companies,' are the ones making the choices and that their personal orientations as well as their place in the power and leadership structure of the firm matters (Prakash, 2000). Others call for greater attention to managers' commitment, perceptions, and leadership in explaining how they interpret external pressures for environmental performance (Coglianese and Nash, 2001; Andersson and Bateman, 2000; Sharma, 2000; Forbes and Jermier, 2002).

This search to open up the 'black box' of the organization and peer into its internal workings, power structure, incentives and the motivations of its decision-makers is certainly a move in the right direction. Indeed, one empirical study found that managers' 'environmental management style' was a better predictor of environmental performance than were external regulatory, economic, and social pressures (Gunningham *et al.*, 2003). Another study of closely matched pairs of facilities suggests that choices to participate or not in a government-run voluntary environmental program stem from a constellation of managers' perceptions and motivations, including their trust in regulators, and incentives within their corporation (Howard-Grenville *et al.*, 2006).

Without a sense of where managerial perceptions, style or interpretations come from, and how they may be altered, however, this inquiry into internal factors may produce little more than a 'laundry list.' Additional items will be added to the already long list of possible factors – external regulatory, social and economic conditions – that *can* shape the environmental actions of a given firm or facility. Managerial style, or managerial perceptions may simply become catchphrases to explain away the unexplainable – the seemingly idiosyncratic differences between companies' actions in the face of similar external pressures. The utility of such constructs risks getting lost, just as some warned that the popularity of the construct of organizational culture would reduce it to 'an empty, if entertaining, catch-all construct explaining everything and nothing' (Allaire and Firsirotu, 1984: 194).

In order to avoid being forever a vague, fuzzy, abstract concept, culture has taken on concrete meaning through the close description and analysis of particular cultures (Weeks, 2004). Similarly, the close description and analysis of how managers within a company approach and advance environmental issues can bring concrete meaning to constructs like environmental management style. The hunch that a variety of internal factors shape particular choices and actions on environmental issues is a good one; the tools that help us follow this hunch can be provided by the literature on culture.

ORGANIZATIONAL CULTURE, INTERPRETATION, AND ACTION

Culture has been a prominent concept in organizational research for more than two decades, but there has long been and remains considerable variation in how researchers view and study culture (Smircich, 1983; Martin, 2002; Weeks, 2004). While some view culture as a variable that can be manipulated to produce various organizational outcomes, others view it as 'a root metaphor for conceptualizing organization' (Smircich, 1983: 342). In the latter case, culture is something an organization 'is,' rather than something it 'has' (Smircich, 1983). I adopt the latter, interpretive perspective on culture, and view culture as a pattern of meanings (Geertz, 1973) that are represented and recreated through actions and artifacts. This builds on Gregory's definition of culture as 'a system of meanings that accompany the myriad behaviors and practices recognized as a distinct way of life' (1983: 364) and acknowledges that several types of evidence – artifacts, behaviors, and interactions – are pieced together to yield a 'multi-faceted and complex picture of the various kinds of symbol systems and their associated meanings' (Smircich, 1983: 351). This view of culture encompasses ideas (beliefs, meanings) and material aspects (symbols, artifacts) as well as the actions that members of an organization take that respond to and recreate these meanings (Jermier *et al.*, 1991; Riley, 1983; Weeks and Galunic, 2003).

While culture brings together action, artifacts, and meanings, it is not immediately clear from these definitions where these come from, and why they may differ between groups or organizations. We can observe a distinct pattern of meanings within a culture, but if we cannot explain at least partially where the pattern came from, why it persists, and why it might differ from that found in another culture, we do nothing to move cultural explanations away from the realm of the idiosyncratic. Anthropologist Mary Douglas dismissed the notion that 'culture was its own explanation' that could justify 'otherwise arbitrary restrictions and permissions arising from within its patterns' (Douglas, 1978: 1). She sought to develop a scheme that related the patterns of social relations found in a group to the 'cosmology' – beliefs about the nature of the world – of its members.

Cultural Bias

Douglas's notion of 'cultural bias' suggests that beliefs are 'locked together into relational patterns' and are informed by the degree and forms of social control exercised within a culture (1978: 14). For example, she argues that hierarchical cultures, in which individuals experience strong boundaries and rules govern internal specialization and interaction, will see in nature 'similarities and regularities' (Douglas, 1978: 23). Nature, for hierarchical cultures, can and should be managed within boundaries; it is not fragile unless pushed too far. An individualist culture where individuals feel bound by neither group membership nor role classification will tend to view nature as benign and relatively robust; nature will recover from any perturbations on its own, according to such cultures (Thompson *et al.*, 1990; Douglas 1992c). Similarly, Douglas identifies beliefs about time, human nature, and justice that are consistent with four generic forms of social organization (1978: 22–36). While the scheme risks being seen as overly deterministic, Douglas notes that: 'the chains of cause and effect between the structures of social interaction and cosmological and cultural system which are supporting them are indefinitely interwoven and interdependent' (1978: 53).

Like many theories which reduce a great diversity of situations to several key variables, Douglas's scheme is primarily useful as a heuristic device. It suggests that patterns of interaction shape how individuals in a culture view themselves and that which lies beyond their boundaries. It asserts that beliefs about the physical environment tend to travel in self-consistent packages with other beliefs, including those about time, human nature, justice and danger. Cultural bias does not suggest that some cultures have distorted views of the world; it does suggest that all cultures, by virtue of being cultures – webs of meaning spun by their members – pay attention to some things and ignore others, count some things as 'in' and others as 'out.' And it points toward looking at action and interaction – what I take to be the work within an organization and the organization of this work – as a starting point for understanding these categorizations.

Problem Setting and Strategies for Action

As systems of meaning, then, cultures are also schemes of classification that shape what their members may pay attention to and what they ignore (Douglas, 1978), what they count as 'normal' and what they do not (Douglas, 1966). Cultural meanings and categories contribute to how individuals 'set' problems, a process which occurs, according to Schön, as 'we select what we will treat as the "things" of the situation, we set the boundaries of our attention to it, and we impose upon it a coherence which allows us to say what is wrong and in what directions the situation needs to be changed' (Schön, 1983: 40).

Problem setting suggests that, from a wide range of possible issues, certain environmental problems will be selected by members of an organization and certain schemes will be invoked to categorize these problems. In other words, the cultural categories that are ready at hand to organizational members filter issues from the natural environment such that some become problems and others do not. What are these categories, and where might they come from? Such categories emerge from the familiar and repeated actions that are central to the work of the organization. Indeed, research shows that existing organizational categories are invoked to frame environmental problems as ones of product quality, cost control, customer care, or social responsibility (Crane, 2000; Starkey and Crane, 2003; Howard-Grenville and Hoffman, 2003).

But ready at hand categories for setting problems are not the only consequence of organizational cultures. Sociologist Anne Swidler argues that 'the significance of specific cultural symbols can be understood only in relation to the strategies of action they sustain' (1986: 283). Strategies for action are neither consciously developed anew by individuals contemplating a certain problem, nor are they forced upon individuals by the culture. Instead, individuals construct strategies for action using at least some 'pre-fabricated links' and culture 'influences action through the shape and organization of those links' (Swidler, 1986: 277). In this sense, culture is 'more like a "toolkit" or repertoire . . . from which actors select differing pieces for constructing lines of action' (Swidler, 1986: 277).

Even though individuals can always bend the rules within an organizational culture, certain strategies for action tend to persist (Howard-Grenville, 2005). Furthermore, the ends to which these strategies are applied may not be consciously scrutinized. If the typical solution for a particular problem is to run a focus group, for example, then the information obtained from such an exercise will be valued, even if the focus group in some cases is not actually an optimal solution to the problem. Members of a culture tend to value the outcomes that their strategies are most suited to attain (Swidler, 1986), suggesting a reciprocal relationship between the interpretations, or problem setting, that a culture sustains and the actions its members engage in. In other words, actions are informed by the nature of problems, and they, in turn, reinforce categories of problems by reproducing distinctions between problems that are solvable and those that are not. In this way, attention to issues and actions on them are closely linked.

As Schön (1983) argued, the very act of selecting the 'things' of a situation invokes diagnoses (what is wrong?) and prescriptions (what needs to be done?). But experience with diagnosis and prescription can limit and focus the 'things' that pop out as salient in the next situation.

The Organization of Culture

Anyone with experience in organizations knows that organizational cultures are rarely monolithic. As Weeks points out, 'culture is socially distributed across the organization – and unevenly so' (2004: 55). Different subcultures can form around occupational groupings, organizational roles, hierarchical levels, and functional or professional identifications, and they emerge around shared understandings of tasks, mission and authority structures (Van Maanen and Barley, 1985; Jermier *et al.*, 1991; Schein, 1996; Stevenson and Bartunek, 1996; Hofstede, 1998). Differentiation between subcultures may be more the norm than the exception in companies (Schein, 1996; Martin, 2002). In fact, an overall organizational culture may not simply be differentiated around several otherwise cohesive subcultures, it may actually be fragmented, with ambiguity regarding cultural meanings a permanent and accepted part of organizational life (Meyerson and Martin, 1987; Martin, 2002).

The image of organizations as multicultural (Gregory, 1983), and only rarely sharing a single, overarching system of meanings, considerably complicates the role of culture in shaping problem setting and strategies for action. In fact, one aspect that defines an organizational subculture is that the members 'share a set of problems commonly defined to be the problems of all, and routinely take actions on the basis of collective understandings unique to the group' (Van Maanen and Barley, 1985: 38). If an organization is comprised of multiple, perhaps cross-cutting, subcultures then whose problem interpretations and actions will matter, and will some interpretations and strategies for actions trump others? In other words, who gets a say in defining what environmental problems are and how they will be acted upon? Many voices may be heard, but only some will prevail in the subsequent negotiation and contestation.

If subcultures are differentiated, that is 'each subculture is an island of localized lucidity, so that ambiguity lies only in the interstices among the subcultures' (Meyerson and Martin, 1987: 633), then one type of outcome may result. Each subculture might be well adapted to enacting and responding to 'its' portion of the organization's issues and environment, yet loosely coupled with other subcultures within the organization (Lawrence and Lorsch, 1967; Meyerson and Martin, 1987). Put in terms of problem setting and strategies for action, differentiated subcultures would have their own, and presumably appropriate to the task, categories for interpreting problems and preferred strategies for action, and these might not overlap those of other subcultures. Members of a subculture would select and attend to 'their' aspects of a given environmental issue, adopting strategies for action from their own repertoire.

If subcultures are fragmented, the consequences for setting and solving problems might be quite different. In fragmented organizational cultures differences in meanings and behavioral norms are incommensurable or irreconcilable (Meyerson and Martin, 1987) and even subcultural boundaries are hard to draw because sources of connection and difference between subcultures are animated through particular issues, with the issues themselves transient (Meyerson and Martin, 1987). In this case, problem setting and strategies for action might appear relatively arbitrary, enacted in response to a particular issue, the context in which that issue has arisen, and the set of players involved.

Another possibility is that the distribution of culture within an organization is not adequately captured by regarding groups as subcultures. Culture, and subcultures, need to have shared some history long enough for patterns of meaning and action to have emerged (Schein, 1996). What happens when new groups are formed, or when projects or work teams bring together individuals from a variety of other groups? What happens when a new group encounters a long established group that may well operate as a distinct subculture? Whether we call these groups subcultures or not, the organization of culture within and between them matters to how they interact.

Power, Culture and 'Selling' Issues

How are differences between subcultures – or groups within an organization where culture is unevenly distributed – reconciled? Whose interpretations and actions trump those of others if an organization's culture is differentiated or even fragmented? Even within the literature on subcultures, little attention has been paid to the relative power of subcultures, although several scholars note implicitly or explicitly that subcultures are not equally powerful (Jermier *et al.*, 1991; Kunda, 1992; Bloor and Dawson, 1994; Stevenson and Bartunek, 1996).

Questions of relative power become important when we focus on the ongoing interaction of meaning, interpretations and actions between groups. Meanings are always animated and sustained through power structures (Giddens, 1984); they are 'contingent claims which have to be sustained and "made to count" ' (ibid.: 30). In other words, the meanings and cultural categories held by some groups hold greater sway than those of others. New groups, or less powerful subcultures, cannot simply impose their meanings on others. Interactions between groups with different histories or different command over cultural categories may be more about legitimizing new concerns and getting action on them than they are about having another group internalize a particular set of norms (Perrow, 1972; Bloor and Dawson, 1994). Groups seeking to advance new problems and new strategies for action within an organization may well not 'change the minds' of others but instead seek to influence others by connecting new issues to existing types of problems and strategies.

A large body of work addresses how individuals and groups exercise influence within organizations, but it previously has not addressed cultural or subcultural norms and categories, nor differences in power between groups. Prominent influence behaviors include the use of rational persuasion, presenting issues using data and sound business logic, involving others and persistence (Kipnis *et al.*, 1980; Yukl and Falbe, 1990; Dutton and Ashford, 1993). 'Issue selling' is a particular type of influence behavior defined as 'the process by which individuals affect others' attention to and understanding of events, developments, and trends that have implications for organizational performance' (Dutton *et al.*, 2001). While it initially focused on bottom-up efforts – that is, attracting the attention of senior management – the concept of issue selling is now being applied to efforts to gain attention and action on issues across the organization, between peers or between people in different functional groups (Bansal, 2003).

In order to understand issue selling across organizations, however, it is critical to understand how differences in meanings or cultural categories between issue sellers and recipients influence their interaction and its outcomes. Both constraints and opportunities are present. Recipients may simply not 'get it' when others try to advance issues that are couched in specialized, unfamiliar language. Or they may treat the issues as unimportant even if they understand them and appreciate the differences they represent. These are common pitfalls when people from different groups try to bring together specialized knowledge and interests. In such circumstances, they frequently differ not only in terms of what they know, but how they know it and how they value it (Dougherty, 1992; Carlile, 2002; Bechky, 2003). However, the opportunities in such cases arise when people can creatively and skillfully use their relationships, their knowledge of how a group or the organization as a whole works, and/or their past experience, to tap into meanings and categories that resonate with others (Dutton *et al.*, 2001; Feldman, 2004). Such opportunities are 'local,' in the sense that they must be taken around particular interactions on particular issues, rather than sought globally across a broad, generic set of issues. They may also be fleeting, with windows of opportunity opening and closing unpredictably, suggesting that those who seek to advance issues may do so opportunistically. Finally, differences that arise in earlier interactions may be taken as sources of learning – about important cultural categories, for example – that can be used to improve efforts and outcomes on later interactions.

Cultural differences are an impediment to those seeking to advance a new issue in a company, but issue sellers *do* operate effectively from positions of hierarchical, political or cultural disadvantage (Ashford *et al.*, 1998; Dutton *et al.*, 2001; Dutton *et al.*, 2002). Exactly how they do so is not well understood. How do issue sellers learn about the cultural categories that are meaningful to their audience? How do they represent issues so they are regarded as problems or concerns of these groups? And how do such representations tap into the strategies for action favored by such groups? These questions are taken up in the following chapters through a close examination of Tech and environmental work at Chipco, a shift in how environmental work was represented over time, and associated outcomes.

SUMMARIZING THE CONCEPTUAL JOURNEY

To sum up: Ideas of nature and the environment are not singular. Both carry multiple interpretations, none of which can claim to be wholly true or correct, but all of which sustain certain prescriptions for action. By extension, we should not expect companies or the decision-makers within them to hold singular views of what constitutes an important environmental issue, who is responsible, and what must be done about it. Until relatively recently, however, regulatory and other actions designed to elicit certain levels of environmental performance paid little or no attention to how those within companies perceived environmental issues. Similarly, scholarship on corporate environmental management was largely unconcerned with the internal workings of firms. The strategic tradition focused on what companies ought to do under certain competitive conditions, the sociological tradition focused on what companies did do as the 'rules of the game' shifted. Neither approach offered much help in understanding why individual firms often acted quite differently under similar conditions.

The latter part of the chapter argued that internal factors matter to how members of a company interpret and act on environmental issues. But rather than rely on loose constructs such as environmental management style, it introduced organizational culture as a starting point for describing and assessing how internal factors – the work of an organization, and its organization of work – influence its actions. Cultures are interpretive structures – webs of meaning sustained by their members – that are reproduced through the social processes of action and interaction. Culture categories help to sort out what types of problems are treated as the norm, and what types of solutions are invoked to fix them. But lest culture be seen as a simple force, we must recognize differences between groups within any company. Different functional groups, or groups with differing histories, locations and so on, may develop quite different cultures. They also may exercise quite different power within the company as a whole. The challenge then, is not only to understand how a company's culture shapes its attention and action on environmental issues, but to consider how individuals and groups within a company navigate and negotiate the uneven distribution of cultural meaning. Who gets the say on how a particular issue is interpreted? And how can those who have little historical say on such matters sell their interpretations of issues? The Chipco analysis does not speak to how all corporate cultures shape attention and action on environmental issues, but it does open up the black box now labeled 'managerial style' to considerably enrich understanding of how the internal workings of a company influence its environmental actions.

NOTE

1. In 1993, *Fortune* magazine published an article ranking the ten leaders and ten laggards on environmental issues. The criteria used to determine the rankings included toxic releases, percentage reductions in toxic releases, and an assessment of the comprehensiveness of the company's environmental practices (Hoffman, 2000: 116).

4. 'Tech' work at Chipco

> [Chipco] tends to focus on things that limit performance, the whole corporate psyche is around problem-solving.
>
> Chipco manager

My initial encounter with work plans, related in Chapter 2, was only the first time I saw how important planning and measurement was to the management of people and projects at Chipco. Through that incident, and in experiencing daily life at Chipco, I gained the sense that no decision was arbitrary, no conclusion arrived at without relying on data. But this penchant for planning, goals and measurement may suggest that the organization put a high value on the act of planning for its own sake. Nothing could be further from the truth. Planning was necessary, and tolerated, only to the extent that it served a higher goal: action. Executing one's plans, completing one's ARs, making the manufacturing machine better, and keeping it running were the things that ultimately counted, particularly to the groups involved in manufacturing process development ('Tech') and manufacturing itself ('Manufacturing'). This chapter explores planning and action in these groups, its modes and forms, and the ends it served. It describes what constitutes daily work for members of these groups and from this draws out cultural meanings associated with the physical world, individual roles and interactions, knowledge and time. These cultural meanings provide a basis for comparison with those associated with environmental work at Chipco and give a sense of what members engaged in such work encountered as they tried to influence the core work of manufacturing process development.

ORIENTED TO ACTION

Early in my time at Chipco, I participated in my first BUM (Business Update Meeting). Attendance at these quarterly meetings was mandatory for all employees and they were scheduled to accommodate all shifts. Nonetheless, if an employee had to miss a BUM given by her own group's management, she was encouraged to attend one presented by another group. It was under these circumstances that I joined roughly 400 Tech engineers, technicians and managers filing into a darkened auditorium one morning. Before this standing-room-only crowd, the director of Tech presided over the presentations, first showing several professionally produced videos describing Chipco's business conditions and overall performance. Charts, graphs and tables showed everything from the financial performance of the company and its different divisions, to market growth in various geographical regions, the timing of new product launches, and technical parameters associated with new process development and factory performance. Senior executives appeared in the videos to highlight particular challenges or accomplishments, but, regardless of how strong the previous quarter's results were, they invariably warned against complacency.

The Tech director's own data were then added. Slides showed the capacity of factories, the yields achieved, the rate at which wafers were being processed, and measures of line width and transistor speed which indicated how well the process under development was performing. To my untrained ear, much of this information sounded like a foreign code, with metrics of 'WIP,' 'ISO' and 'wspw.' But trends were clear. Numerical goals had been established in advance and performance against them was now being ranked. While four key Tech goals had been met, another four had not. This was only an interim review, however, and, with employee bonuses tied to the group's accomplishment of these goals, the priorities for the next few months were made clear. Concluding the BUM, the Tech director entertained a handful of questions from the audience and then briskly wrapped up the hour-and-a-half session by declaring 'back to work!' Earlier in the meeting, after reporting that Chipco's revenues had been flat for more than a year the Tech director had warned that there would be no 'slack' for planning in this year, everyone must 'execute.' Several hundred people filed out of the auditorium to do just that.

Action and Execution: Making Chips and Making them Better

Designing a new generation of manufacturing processes for Chipco is a big job. Like other leading semiconductor manufacturers, Chipco significantly updates its state-of-the-art fabrication facilities, or 'fabs,' every two years to enable the production of faster, more powerful chips. A typical manufacturing fab has a 100 000-square-foot 'clean room' filled with dozens of sets of 'tools' to perform hundreds of process steps. Despite their size and complexity, the pieces of equipment used to manufacture chips were consistently referred to as 'tools.' Hammers these were not. A typical tool easily exceeded the size of a refrigerator, and many were the size of minivans or larger. One new tool for a critical process step could cost several hundred thousand dollars; a typical fab would need a dozen of each type. The capital investment to equip a new fab ran into billions of dollars.

Tech's job was to test, modify and optimize tools and procedures at a dedicated development fab in order to establish the myriad detailed parameters for each new manufacturing process generation. Roughly one-third of the hundreds of process steps required to make a chip underwent a major change (for example, new tool adopted) and many of the remaining steps underwent some significant change (for example, the same tool but new operating parameters, new chemicals or gases) on a relentless two year development cycle. The goal was to improve critical process steps or 'modules' to enable a significant reduction in the size of chip components and circuitry, and a concomitant improvement in chip speed.

Once the modules of a new process generation were developed by Tech, they were scaled up to operate at higher volume and then rolled out sequentially to several manufacturing fabs. The entire 'ramp' for a new manufacturing process could span a year, as some fabs continued to operate the previous process generation, retiring and replacing it on a schedule that accounted for the economics of the two generations and the demand for the chips they produced. The Tech development fab was where it all began; decisions made here perpetuated through as many as seven manufacturing fabs, each of which was regarded as part of a seamless 'virtual fab,' united by identical process tools, operating with identical parameters, using identical input and process materials, and producing, with identical yield, identical chips. Indeed, the goal of the virtual fab was to make it impossible to discern a chip made in New Mexico from one made in New England, or even – had a fab been located there – New Delhi.

TECH AND THE PHYSICAL WORLD: ACTION ON THE INSIDE

With all this at stake, my concerns prior to my first excursion into the Tech fab were much more mundane: getting dressed. 'Gowning up' is not simply a condition of entry to a fab; the speed and skill with which one can pull it off are a strong signal of technical competence. One Tech engineer who had been unusually accommodating of an engineer from another group, coaching him in the ways of Tech, and taking him into the fab to learn about relevant equipment, shook his head in frustration when he told me that, 'it still took him 15 minutes to get dressed.' A Tech engineer or technician who works regularly in the fab can gown up in under five minutes. As there is only one gowning room to enter the fab, the procedure is quite public, and those who fumble stand out.

Gowning Up and Getting In

I was well aware of this when I was accompanied into the Tech fab by Matt,[1] a technician from my group. He patiently instructed me in the correct steps and cheerfully nodded and waved to his peers as they breezed through the procedure. Matt told me he used to gown up in four minutes when he was working in the fab every day. Now he rarely goes in, and is up to eight minutes. In the hall outside the entrance to the gowning room we each donned a disposable hair net, checking the mirror to push in any stray hairs. A drink from the adjacent water fountain was next, to 'settle the particles' in our mouths. (Someone later told me that step is designed for smokers, but any rule must be applied consistently.) Immediately upon entry there was a station with presaturated disposable wipes used to clean pagers and ID badges brought from the outside. Then we grabbed pairs of blue disposable booties and sat down on a bench. These were slipped on over our shoes as we swung our legs, one after the other, from the 'dirty' side of the bench to the clean side. Thin nylon gloves came next, offered in a wide array of men's and women's sizes.

Those infrequently in the fab choose a 'bunny suit' from the sizes arrayed in a number of bins at eye level; regulars have their own suits, helmets and safety glasses waiting on a hanger. We both found our size from the bins and removed the suit from its plastic bag. Try as I could to step into it without letting any portion of it touch the floor, as I had been instructed, I did manage to drag one leg on the floor, then step on it with the foot of the leg already in the suit. As if I didn't already feel out of place, this clearly signaled that I was a novice. I trusted that my clean blue booties had minimally soiled the thick, white Gore-Tex fabric of the suit, and continued to pull it on, fully covering my arms, legs, and torso and zipped it up at either side of my neck. A nylon head covering, balaclava-style, came next and was tucked into the neck of the suit, followed by a hard plastic helmet with a clear face shield. A small filter unit attached with its batteries to a belt and was hooked to the helmet to suck out and clean expired air. Moving closer to the door of the fab, we stopped at a second bench where we repeated the move to swing our legs over to the clean side as we pulled on one tall boot and then the next. Made of a similar white fabric to the suits, these had soft rubber soles and strapped tight just under the knee. We then donned safety goggles and a second pair of gloves, made of thin latex, that we tucked into our bunny suit sleeves.

Despite the breathability of the Gore-Tex, I was already starting to perspire when we stepped through the clean room door. The world became a deep, enveloping amber. The orange-yellow lights overhead branched off in only a few sections, where light sensitive chemicals were not used, to a normal fluorescent glow. For a factory, the place was disarmingly silent. The hum of air filtration systems, which produced a vertical flow of air from ceiling to floor, and fully replaced the clean room air every ten minutes, was the predominant sound. Adjusting to this new environment, fully clothed head to toe in what was the closest I'd ever come to wearing space gear, I began to feel slightly disoriented. I glanced around for the closest chair or stool in case I needed to sit down. Very few were in evidence, but I made a mental note of their location as I took a deep breath to calm my dizziness.

Creating Chips

Perhaps most alarming to me, as we moved through various areas in the fab, careful not to get in the way of others in bunny suits walking purposively around or monitoring the operation of various tools, was the fact that the chips were almost invisible. They were there, but largely seen only as 'boats' of wafers sliding silently by on automated tracks above our heads. Each black plastic boat held a batch of 25 wafers, and lids protected them from light and other forms of contamination. Each wafer, a thin circle of extremely pure silicon, roughly the size of a plate, could hold several hundred individual chips that were built up on a minute layer on its surface. Four to six weeks of processing were needed to create a chip from start to finish. A code on each wafer included all the information about its journey through the process so far. The wafer movements could be tracked and controlled remotely. An engineer can check on the status of a wafer lot from home at midnight by logging on from a laptop computer. The engineer can type in a few lines of code, and with the assistance of a technician in the fab moving boats from staging areas to tools, have the wafers stop, start or change their journey through the process steps.

The tools themselves typically had black, clean fronts that made them look more like massive microwave ovens with control consoles than like advanced technical systems that were patterning, depositing, etching or heating wafers to alter their electronic properties on a minute scale. The gases and chemicals needed to make this happen were plumbed in invisibly from the back; waste similarly disappeared through pipes that were largely hidden from view. Wet benches, where wafers were cleaned between certain process steps by being dipped into a series of acid baths, were the most familiar pieces of equipment, and their workings were relatively obvious. Here, robot arms slid along at waist height, lowering and raising open wafer boats into and out of the sinks. In older processes, Matt noted, the benches were not automated, but human differences in lifting and lowering rates were now too great for today's process tolerances. Seconds made a difference to the outcome. Only once did I see a Tech engineer lift and move a single wafer using a suction wand. The stakes were high, because a dropped wafer would shatter like glass plate, one that was worth as much as $30 000.

Matt stopped and rubbed his gloved fingers together near a small black machine, which suddenly came alive, its red lights twinkling. A particle monitor, he pointed out, to alert fab workers to contamination. With smaller and smaller 'features,' or electronic components, being created on chips, contamination control became increasingly critical. A single speck of dust, flake of skin, or human hair could wipe out a whole chip. Our bunny suits were not to protect us from the manufacturing process, but to protect the chips from us. Indeed, we were just big, walking sources of contagion and equipment was hard at work to purge our effects. Three stories of equipment (two above and one below) were used to support a one story clean room. Air filtration and return equipment ensured that air in the clean room had on average less than one particle of dust in a cubic foot, compared to about a million particles in a cubic foot of average room air. Systems that delivered ultra-pure water and gases ensured that contamination was not introduced by the process materials that touched the wafers.

Heading back to the gowning room along the main hall of the fab we veered around a yellow triangular plastic sign, of the kind set out by janitorial employees when they wash a bathroom floor. Indeed, here were janitorial employees, gowned head to toe in bunny suits as other workers in the fab. They were silently mopping with large, flat mops covered with white lint-free cloths. Shrouded in the amber glow of the lights, shielded by their helmets, and with no hint of hair or skin showing, they looked somewhat alien. But they were doing the most mundane and normal task I'd seen in the fab all morning, cleaning the clean room floor. Another defense against contamination.

Summary: Tech and the Physical World

The physical world that members of Tech engage in their work is tightly bounded, highly manipulable and precisely controllable. The boundary between the order of the fab and the outside is clearly delineated both physically – in the walls that separated the clean room from everything else, and the bunny suits worn to prevent workers' hair, skin or breath from contaminating the chips – and procedurally – through the strict gowning up routine to enter the fab. Different people coped with their time in the clean room in different ways. Some limited how much coffee they drank so they wouldn't have to ungown and leave the fab mid-morning for a bathroom break – the disruption of exit and entry was simply too great. Others wore shorts year round to stay comfortable inside a bunny suit. The feeling I had that the clean room was a world apart was perhaps heightened by its novelty for me. Had I been in there daily, I would no doubt have adjusted to its amber color, its lack of windows, and its silent, clean, hard surfaces.

But there is no doubt that the clean room remained physically different from other spaces. I was once sitting at a meeting in the cafeteria with its wall of windows when the fab was 'dumped,' or suddenly evacuated. Dozens of bunny-suited people poured from emergency exit doors onto the grassy area between the buildings, blinking as if disoriented by the bright sunshine on the spring day. While dumping the fab was an infrequent event, it was not unheard of, especially for the Tech fab where experiments were always being run and could result in an 'excursion' like the release of a gas. The sudden disgorging of this ultra-clean place, its carefully clad workers spewed onto the grass (their bunny suits, etc. would be sent straight for special laundering), represented an abrupt cessation of action.

The boundary between the clean room and elsewhere was so critical to maintain because it enabled the highly precise work of chip manufacturing. Work in Tech involved routinely constructing, with great precision, structures not visible to the naked eye. The circuit features on a state-of-the-art chip (at the time of this study) were created by manipulating matter into structures more than 500 times narrower than the width of a human hair, or roughly one-fifth of a micron. These structures were created within tolerances of at least 10 percent, or roughly one-fiftieth of a micron. The necessary precision was achieved through a combination of advanced process design, automation and maintaining the exquisitely clean manufacturing environment I observed. Cleanliness, seen culturally, is simply a statement about order and control. Dirt is a word for 'all the rejected elements of ordered systems' (Douglas, 1966: 35). To Tech engineers, the physical world encountered daily was not simply clean and orange, but also controllable, subject to ordering influences, and ultimately knowable on an intimate scale.

TECH ROLES AND INTERACTIONS ORDERING WORK

Just as work inside the fab was precise and controllable, the planning and ordering of work, and specification of roles and interactions, was highly structured within Tech and throughout Chipco in general. Work was ordered to establish and meet goals, reduce uncertainty, and provide focus for each group or individual. In Tech, work was highly specialized around particular roles delineated by the technology itself and interaction was relatively limited. Interdependencies were managed through agreement on measurable and relatively near-term deliverables, and through the use of bodies dedicated to coordination.

Chipco is not a 'people company' like some others, a Tech manager once told me. He complained about the bureaucracy and formalism, suggesting wryly that 'pretty soon I won't be able to go to the bathroom without getting approval from [the Tech director] and getting a form signed by [his administrative assistant].' What kept him there? That was easy. Chipco paid him well to do what he loved, 'using equipment, gathering data, and understanding stuff.' Members of Tech thrived on difficult technical challenges, but their work was organized to channel innovation and experimentation toward closely prescribed goals and according to carefully developed decision processes.

Results, and More Results

Steve, a manager with the unique responsibility for people development, not process development, within Tech explained that work in Tech follows an 'algorithm.' Improvement in the process is incremental, and certain rules are followed, for example, a certain percentage of equipment from the previous process generation must be reused in the next generation. Contrasting the work environment with that of a research organization where he used to work, Steve noted that, there, many projects were pursued with the expectation that a very few would be fruitful; creativity was encouraged and even failed projects treated as valuable for learning. At Tech, one direction is picked and 'failure is not an option,' he observed. Indeed, the daily activities of Tech engineers are expected to lead directly to results – working process modules. Some engineers were rotated through stints in a small, 'innovative' group in Tech, where the work was focused not on the next manufacturing process, but on the one beyond that. But their stay in this group was temporary because, as one manager explained, to progress in their careers the engineers need to be 'producing daily results, otherwise it will hurt at the end of the year [review].'

The work, and results, of each engineer in Tech were oriented around 'Module Targets Specs [Specifications],' the technical performance parameters that defined what was acceptable for each process module. According to one engineer, only three things 'count' for him and his peers: 'what your manager says, what your process module specs are, and what your annual performance review said.' Engineers 'all have their blinders on,' he added, to focus exclusively on their part of the process. Indeed, roles were specialized to limit the need for interaction between engineers.

The technology itself defines roles, with certain engineers and technicians specialized on certain process steps and equipment and further specialized by the layer of the chip. For example, there are many lithography engineers who use the equipment that transfers circuit patterns onto the surface of a wafer, but they are further divided into groups who work on patterning a single layer of the numerous layers needed to produce a finished chip. A given 'litho' engineer often had little or no work-related interaction with another litho engineer who worked on a different chip layer, or with a polish engineer who worked on the same chip layer.

Coordination for Results

With focus and specialization so coveted, coordination was also deliberate and explicit. Daily and weekly rituals structured work in an immediate fashion. In the manufacturing fabs and the Tech fab, twice daily 'pass-downs' were held. At 7 a.m. and 7 p.m., tool 'owners' coming off their 12-hour shift met with those coming on. Tool performance, status of WIP ('Work In Progress'), and any problems or excursions from normal operating conditions were discussed. The meetings took place in the fab with members clothed in bunny suits gathered around the tool. The next meeting of the day, 30 minutes later, transferred this information up to the level of the operations managers, who were responsible for overall factory performance and output. These more senior managers also gowned up in bunny suits and assembled in a clean conference room inside the fab. Instead of just being a one-way conduit for information, these meetings accomplished the ordering of work in the fab for the following 12 hours. Priorities were assigned, marching orders issued.

Weekly written reports were required of all employees, whether they worked in a fab or not. Each person's 'weekly' was sent to his or her manager, who consolidated them and passed a single weekly along to the next level of management, and so on. Mastering the genre of a good weekly was not difficult; brevity was encouraged, data or results coveted. Bullet points or headings might delineate the results obtained from multiple activities. And, my manager advised, weeklies should contain both 'highlights and lowlights.' What results have you obtained this week, what problems have you encountered?

Coordination also occurred much more formally, with many Tech managers dedicating a significant portion of their time to evaluating data on the process under development, reviewing recommendations for tools or procedures, and formally ratifying these decisions through multiple decision-making and approval bodies. One pervasive coordinating body, the TechCouncil, was a key forum for making decisions that influenced the trajectory of a set of process technologies. More than ten such Councils operated at Chipco, with the first ones initiated in Tech. Their members made decisions about process development, as well as materials use, factory support systems, factory automation, and environmental impacts and natural resource use. The Councils were intentionally kept small and membership limited to those who were, in the words of one TechCouncil chair, 'empowered to make the decisions and to take them back and drive them in their organizations.' She quickly added that such meetings were 'not just an FYI.'

The work of TechCouncils and other decision-making and approval bodies was also oriented to produce results. Agendas for such meetings often specified more than just the time, topic and presenter. They had a column for the 'expected outcome' of a presentation – for example, 'ratification' or 'information and feedback.' An 'AR tracking' page was attached to the back of the agenda to summarize 'Actions Required' that were identified at an earlier meeting, the AR's 'owner,' and the date it was 'due.' So pervasive was this orientation to work as action toward results that the chair of one TechCouncil explained the body's work to me by first saying, 'I just looked at my horizon projects for the next year and there are about 60 decisions that need to be made for [my process area].' The number of decisions would serve as an important measure of the group's work.

Measurement as Management

Measurement and quantification perhaps came easily and naturally to those I encountered at Chipco, for the majority were engineers, technicians, or Ph.Ds by training. Individual and group goals, process and design parameters, experimental results, and work outputs were invariably presented numerically. Take for, example, one of five annual goals for the Tech group to 'maintain and grow the [Tech] edge by enhanced assimilation training and improved culture survey results.' A goal was established for a 10 percent improvement in culture survey results, and for 85 percent employee participation in the survey. To enable the participation goals, mandatory meetings were set up by work groups at which individuals would complete the survey. Several months later, those implementing the survey were pleased to report at a mandatory all-Tech meeting that a 12 percent improvement in culture survey scores had been attained, and, further, that Tech's culture scores were 10 percent higher than the Chipco average. Culture seemed to be on track, although improvement opportunities had been identified. The results of the culture survey, while no doubt a useful managerial gauge of employee satisfaction, likely say much less about the actual culture than does the way in which the survey was implemented. Even the cultural was subject to management through measurement.

Daily, measurement played a central role in decision making. One manager observed that Chipco doesn't make decisions based on 'a conjecture about the future.' 'If you say there's an X percent chance of something happening, the TechCouncil would say "come back when you know for sure",' he added. Indeed, few engineers or technicians would dream of making conjectures, or advancing an idea without data. One engineer was trying to convince others that ultra-pure water did the job just as well as a cleaning chemical used by the janitorial staff in the fab. She had done an experiment comparing the drying times of water against the chemical in question, and proudly informed me that the results showed that it took 'only 1.8 percent longer' for water to dry than it took for the chemical to dry. An insignificant difference, to be sure, but a strangely precise portrayal of the data, it struck me. Presumably the technician knew that if she told others the water and chemical had 'about the same drying time' they would respond with a characteristic, frank, 'show me the data.'

Measurement enabled precision and action, which, as in the fab, was prized in seemingly all facets of work at Chipco. One morning I found a piece of paper half the size of an $8\frac{1}{2} \times 11''$ page on my desk. 'Help meet the recycling challenge and save money,' it announced in block capitals. Chipco's sites in the state had established a 55 percent recycling goal for all materials. The paper summarized the facts so far. In the first quarter, the sites had recycled only 48 percent of material. There was a gap between the goal and the actual performance, but the notice pointed out that efforts in the previous six months had resulted in 25.44 tons of recycled material and avoidance of $2798.40 in disposal fees. That wouldn't be about 25 tons and almost $2800.

The point of the message was to inspire those office workers who did not have a desk-side recycling box to call up the 'Action Line' and request one. Those of us who did have a box (and that would be the great majority because the box was standard issue in a cubicle) were presumably supposed to contribute immediately to the goal by tossing the paper in. Later in the week I overheard some of my cubicle neighbors tittering in the aisle about what a waste of paper it had been to print up thousands of recycling announcements and distribute them to every desk, and I was relieved to hear that someone else had noticed the irony of this particular measurement effort.

Summary of Tech Roles and Interactions

Interactions within Tech were highly routinized. The single-minded focus on work objectives virtually excluded any other interactions that might distract from it. Communications in the form of voicemail, email or pager messages went unanswered by Tech engineers unless they were deemed useful to furthering the engineers' own work objectives. Formal mechanisms – pass downs, weeklies and AR tracking – were expected to carry the burden of coordination and communication. The routinization of interaction, and the restriction of access imposed by narrow work focus contribute to what Douglas (1978) calls 'insulation,' a feature of social groups characterized by rule-bound interaction among individuals. Role specialization meant that transactions were not broad and negotiable, but relatively limited in scope and predictable. Assigning engineers and technicians to work on specific tools and specific chip layers created by those tools encouraged the development of distinct and largely non-overlapping areas of expertise, further contributing to insulation.

With an emphasis on the development and widespread deployment internally of numeric metrics, Tech also established and largely controlled its own criteria for success. Data and measurement provided powerful and easily shared goals, and the ability to reach these goals was assumed to be under the control of those within Chipco.

TECH AND KNOWLEDGE: WORKING ON ORDER

The ordering of work, through role specialization, mechanisms for coordination, and an orientation toward measurable results served an important end: reining in uncertainty and inconsistency to create not only working fab processes, but to create them on a strict and aggressive schedule, and replicate them identically across numerous locations. Tech and others within Chipco saw themselves as aggressive and relentless problem solvers. The 'whole corporate psyche is around problem solving,' observed one manager. Independently, a Tech engineer suggested 'our business demands that we do everything on a short term basis and Chipco's success is a result of getting things to work in a short time.' 'We're such good problem solvers that when a problem comes up we'll figure out a way,' another added. And, on a separate occasion a manager who often argued for a less reactive stance, nonetheless admitted that 'problem avoidance is counter cultural' at Chipco.

This stance shaped how those within Tech and Manufacturing understood their work, and ultimately, how those involved in designing and running manufacturing processes regarded the construction of knowledge. Knowledge claims could be substantiated through controlled experimentation and the collection of data. Problems, simply put, were things that didn't work to specification. The knowledge needed to fix a problem was practical knowledge, insight gained by processing test wafers or running other experiments in the fab. 'Make it work' was a phrase heard frequently within Tech, where the focus was always on solutions. One engineer related a meeting with a group manager in which the manager told him to put away the list of technical issues he had brought to discuss. The manager didn't want to hear about problems, he expected certain results and only cared to know whether and how these were obtained.

. . . and Working Hard

The status of Tech within Chipco, and of individuals within Tech, turned on their reputation for obtaining results and implementing solutions. Within Tech 'the critical players are the ones who take on the biggest challenges,' one manager observed. They seemed to reflect a Chipco founder's advice who, asked about lessons for career success, advised 'just be 100 percent concentrated on what you want to do in the period of time you can meaningfully affect.' Tech employees perpetuated an air of superiority relative to other groups – they worked harder, worked smarter, and, according to one manager, simply had more 'work output.' One Tech engineer complained that when he asked an environmental engineer about a chemical he responded, 'what is it?' Had he been a member of Tech, the engineer argued, he would have not only known about the chemical but aggressively sought further information by asking 'is it the –ic form or the –ous form?' and 'what valence is it?'

Members of Tech are so focused and hold each other to high standards because they regard themselves as the fuel for what was described as the manufacturing 'treadmill.' 'The bottom line is that you have to deliver your process module on time, because if there's no new process there's no Chipco,' explained one Tech engineer. If Tech fails, then 'Chipco loses its production edge and someone else catches up,' she added. One student intern, upon learning that I worked physically at the Tech site, said 'I've heard they do *amazing* things over there,' his eyes growing large. Others are less polite in their assessment. People in related groups who work with Tech have been known to call them arrogant, but they always, if grudgingly, admit their respect. Tech gets the job done.

A 'Tech Culture' training class involved an exercise in which students had to identify the group's culture, from a set of cartoons on slides. The selected cartoon, and correct one according to the instructor, a Tech manager, depicted a person standing and staring up at a brick wall with a puzzled look on his face. The next frame showed the person bashing through the wall, bricks flying in all directions. Tech's specialty was the removal of constraints that might limit the development of new manufacturing processes. Other groups worked hard to advance their interests in the face of this, but often with limited success. Reflecting on a decision made in Tech several years earlier to use a process chemical that was three times as costly as a workable alternative, a materials manager suggested that all his group could do to avoid such decisions from Tech was to 'try very hard to stand in their way.'

Reliability and Replication

There is a pragmatic reason for Tech's brute force approach. In working quickly to develop new process modules, almost no stone is left unturned, that is, until the module works. At that point, the next technical challenge is taken on, and the working module is passed, unchanged, along the chain to manufacturing. This produces an odd juxtaposition of aggressive problem solving and fervent conservatism. For example, a Tech engineer had been instructed several years earlier to increase the quantity of a raw material used in one process, to more than twice what previous processes had used. The module was not working effectively, and numerous changes including this one were made in an effort to improve its performance. By the time the actual cause of the problem (which had nothing to do with this material) had been found and fixed, it was too late to change the process 'recipe' to specify that the lower volume of material be used, for it was already advancing toward the manufacturing fabs. Even when the engineer collected data that showed a process performance improvement when the lower volume of material was used, it was too late to force the change. A working process was what counted. Several years later, the engineer reported that all of the fabs were still using the higher volume of material that had been prescribed when the process was transferred.

Chipco's emphasis on identical replication of the process steps in the entire 'virtual fab' meant that no single engineer or technician can make even a minor change to the process. Changes were regarded as too risky for they could alter the performance of the process which had been so carefully tweaked by Tech to obtain high yields. Noting that a recycled chemical would not be acceptable in a process step, despite characteristics identical to the virgin material, a Tech engineer asserted that fab managers would say, 'I don't care what it costs, don't let it touch my wafer!' Indeed, saving money was far less important than maintaining a working process. Another engineer explained why a project undertaken in one fab was, in his view, 'perpetually 12 weeks away [from being implemented].' Even though the project was highly successful, he noted that the fab managers didn't want to risk implementing it. 'If you drop yields . . ., it doesn't matter what money you're saving,' he said. Indeed, fiddling with the process could cost money. According to one manufacturing engineer, a ten-second change in process time on his module would 'affect the virtual fab in a big way and could cost millions of dollars.' Recipes were meant to be followed; improvization was unacceptable.

With consistency so coveted, the most seemingly mundane issues could trigger extensive scrutiny and review. One engineer discovered a minor difference in the set-up of equipment between the development fab and a receiving manufacturing fab. At his fab, the plastic covers on part of a tool were intact, but at the manufacturing fab the covers had been removed. Air flow in the tool was slightly different depending on whether the covers were on or off, but the presence or absence of the covers really made little difference to how the equipment operated. Nonetheless, people feared that the process performance might be impacted. Months of fighting went on over who would do what with their covers. The fab that had removed them was sent off to find them, but couldn't. The fab that hadn't removed them refused to do so. In the end, the engineer reported, the decision was to leave each machine as it was, and to violate Chipco's strong norm of identical replication which, he said, 'took a lot of white papering.'

Making any change to a process running in a manufacturing fab required a 'white paper' approved by the relevant process change control boards (PCCBs) and numerous other affected bodies. The white paper needed to quantify the benefits of the proposed change, and demonstrate, through data, that the risks associated with the change had been absolutely mini- mized. In the case of the project described as 'perpetually 12 weeks away,' the white paper process was relatively simple because the fab involved was running one of the older manufacturing processes and hence the change was considered lower risk. The white paper was also classified as a relatively low 'reliability risk level' (measure of how much the change influences process reliability and outcome) and relatively low on the 'tool sharing' scale (a measure of how strongly the equipment being changed was tied to other fab tools). Even so, the white paper was in its tenth revision, it needed to pass through 12 review and approval bodies before it became final, and the review schedule alone spanned two months.

Summary: Tech and Knowledge

The world of Tech and Manufacturing is a fundamentally knowable world. Collecting data on inputs, outputs and performance informs action in this world. Manipulations can be optimized to yield the best outcome, and knowledge is gained through experimentation. To those engaged in tech- nology development and manufacturing, data represents all that is import- ant about the manufacturing process and the fabs. When enough is known, and controlled, replication is possible. Fabs in different time zones are expected to manufacture a product that is indistinguishable when the physical set-up – down to the length of pipes, settings on identical tools, and floor layouts – is identically replicated.

Of course, as scientists, those involved in technology development and manufacturing do expect the world to show some natural, statistical variation. Events within this normal range are not taken as surprises. For example, despite identical processing conditions some chips from a wafer lot will perform faster than others when tested. Within a range, variation is allowable, and chips are sorted into 'bin splits' based on their actual measured speed. But large excursions, outside a predictable normal distribution, are cause for concern. Process excursions in the fab were dealt with by setting a crack team of engineers on the problem.

Technology development and manufacturing engineers work in a world that can be counted on; it is not capricious, merely complex and data-rich. They can learn its secrets through hard work, divide its tasks among themselves and replicate its results widely. In the ordering of work and the orientation of that work toward the creation of order – predictably working, replicable manufacturing processes – the creativity of engineers at Chipco is bounded. For those working in Tech and Manufacturing, the pain of adherence to pedantry is, for the most part, offset by the thrill of solving hard technical problems. But whatever happened to the founder's call, repeated by Dave in the New Employee Orientation, to be unencumbered by history, and to 'go off and do something wonderful'?

TECH AND TIME: PLANNING AND PACING

The language of planning and the incessant orientation to goal-driven action pervaded daily life at Chipco. Several months into my study, listening to a senior manager explain how his manufacturing support group worked to a seminar full of interns, I was struck by his portrayal of the organization and his place in it. He opened his presentation by explaining that 'organizations are like people, they need a purpose, a direction.' He then spent 20 minutes situating his group within Chipco by running through the mission statements and objectives of each larger group, starting with Chipco's corporate strategic objectives, and ending with those of his own group. 'Every [group] needs to be attuned to the corporate mission and translate that mission into what they do,' he observed.

Individual work, at least on paper, also fit into this scheme. About a month after being blasted for having a vague and unmeasurable work plan, it came time to translate this work plan into 'MBPs' (Management by Plan [goals]) and to marry it to the MBPs of the others in my immediate work group. Confused by the categories in the MBP table we had been given as a guide, I asked for clarification of the distinction between 'Strategic Objectives,' 'Key Strategies' and 'Goals.' The Strategic Objective (SO) was the broadest of the three, but was still a precise statement of outcome. Below each SO were listed several Key Strategies, which, members of my group explained, are the things you plan to do to achieve the SO. Start a Key Strategy with an action word, I was told. A Goal, on the other hand, is the quantifiable result of the Key Strategy being executed. Each Key Strategy had an owner, the person or persons responsible for making it happen, and a target date, by which the owner would achieve the Goal.

While it might appear to be simply a matter of mastering formatting and lingo, translating my work plan into an MBP inserted it into this nested sequence of Goals, SOs, and so forth, that formally defined what people do at Chipco. My group once again revisited our MBPs in the late summer when organizational belt-tightening focused attention on the value of our projects and their fit with the larger group's objectives. The group manager sent a memo out with the SOs for the two larger groups ours was embedded in. 'Our tactics and indicators should in most cases be directly in support of the higher level SOs,' he reminded the group.

Beyond justifying the existence of various groups, and helping individuals and smaller groups symbolically jockey for managerial sanction, this formal planning was embedded in a much grander planning and pacing device, one that, rather than being unencumbered by history, literally marked, paced and produced history within this industry. Moore's Law, which originated from industry founder Gordon Moore's observation about the pace of change in the then infantile semiconductor manufacturing industry has, more than anything else, defined what the industry in general, and Chipco in particular, has done over the past four decades. Moore's Law sketches out what that future promises, but not precisely how to get there. It is, if you will, the ultimate MBP.

Moore and More

In 1965, Gordon Moore noticed that, during the first few years of production of semiconductor chips, the number of transistors on a chip had doubled in a short period of time (1965) . State of the art chips then boasted about 60 electronic components. Moore delivered a speech and boldly projected that this rate of change would continue, resulting in exponential growth in a chip's speed and processing power. Moore's Law, as it has come to be known, states that transistor density on chips doubles every 18–24 months.[2] The intervening decades have demonstrated that the industry has complied with Moore's Law with remarkable accuracy. Currently, new microprocessors sport on the order of half a billion transistors in an area of silicon not much larger than the chips of the 1960's.[3]

Moore's Law is why a computer today costs the same as, or less than, a computer did a decade ago, but the two machines bear little other resemblance. It is why one can buy a greeting card today that has more processing power than the world's largest computers had in 1971 (Malone, 1998). Observers of the information age can't find words to capture the full implications of this technological progress. Calling Moore's Law the 'metronome driving the technology age,' one book celebrating the industry's progress observed,

> If, in 1965, you had known nothing about the forces propelling our civilization except Moore's Law, your predictions about life at the century's end would likely have proven more accurate than with any other combination of indicators. Moore's Law has given us an extraordinary gift: we know how and when the future will arrive . . .
>
> This cycle has become so refined, so enmeshed in our daily lives, that it has become as omnipresent and as deeply felt as the seasons. (Malone 1998: 116)

Surely we don't really feel the impacts of Moore's Law like we feel the seasons, but work at Chipco follows a calendar more firmly anchored in the former than the latter. Moore's Law grounds a ubiquitous process of 'roadmapping,' from which flow specific goals for various groups, and expectations and norms about technology development – its pace and direction – that strongly shape actions in the fabs as well as the design and market timing of new chips.

Mapping the Future

Tech roadmaps are documents that establish trajectories for manufacturing process development, including detailed specifications of tool types and parameters, process performance, process chemical and material requirements, and extremely detailed indicators of chip specifications to be achieved – sometimes layer by layer. But roadmap documents aren't limited to only manufacturing equipment, materials and chip specifications. They are produced throughout Chipco for activities as diverse as factory planning, product development, and even 'people development.'

A roadmap document typically takes the form of a time series running horizontally across the top of the page, and the necessary categories (for example, tool, process or chip specifications desired) running vertically down the left hand side. The table is filled in with names and details of tool types, operating specifications, or process or chip parameters that will be achieved at each time period. Importantly, the time scale on Chipco's roadmaps is delineated in terms of the smallest circuit lines, or nominal feature size, that will appear on future chips. Indeed, the seasons or any other marker of time is unneccessary, for there is a broadly assumed one-to-one correspondence between chip feature size and time. Moore's Law dictates this relationship. In order to increase the density of components on a chip every two years, Moore's Law requires that a given number of components occupy half the area they did in the previous manufacturing generation. In one dimension, that means lines are 0.7 (or the square root of 0.5) times the width of the lines in the previous generation. One Chipco engineer was told jokingly early in his career that senior managers had calculators that were only capable of multiplying by 0.7. This scaling factor guided at a high level the development of all roadmaps, or at least the technical ones.

Roadmapping is also an important mechanism for decision making and coordination. A primary activity of TechCouncils is to own, maintain, and develop roadmaps for specific process areas. Managers involved in this have a very clear map of the current manufacturing process generation in development and, through roadmapping, start to define the less certain regions to the right-hand side of the roadmap document. But projecting too far into the future with a roadmap is considered a waste of time. Commenting on the need for future planning to be 'data driven,' one manager observed 'no one trusts the numbers past two years out.' Nonetheless, roadmapping involved progressively mapping the hinterland, and completing a roadmap entry only once the direction was very clear. There was some room for informed speculation on a roadmap document, but any entry, once 'ratified' by a TechCouncil as 'on the roadmap' became firm. Things that are 'on the roadmap' are things that are expected to happen, barring some massive unforeseen change.

Roadmap decisions directly guide the goals of individual engineers working on process modules, and they influence decisions made on related technology roadmaps. As such, roadmaps define the bounds of legitimate activity. For a given process generation and process step what is 'on the roadmap' is referred to as POR, or 'plan of record.' A tool, or a chemical used in a process step, or a process step itself, can be a POR tool, or a POR chemical or a POR process step. In daily usage, and the label *is* used daily and frequently, POR communicates certainty and intentionality. A POR tool, chemical or process step *will* be used in the next manufacturing process.

The label POR itself is used as a shortcut for describing the status of tools or process approaches. If one inquires about a certain piece of equipment, one is likely to be told, for example, 'its POR for litho in XXX' (meaning it is the selected tool of its type to be used in the lithography process area for the manufacturing process labeled XXX.)[4]. This statement on its own establishes the importance of the equipment, for it reveals that it will ultimately be purchased in large quantities and used in all the fabs. POR is such a commonly used term that it has inspired variations. One engineer new to Tech was surprised to hear another engineer consistently refer to a particular piece of equipment as POS. Eventually he asked what POS stood for. The equipment in question, although it was also POR, was the first of its kind and had a number of quirks that made it unpleasant and tricky to use. POS, the engineer was told, stood for 'piece of shit.'

POR perpetuates through the entire virtual fab. The white papering and change control process described earlier exists to enforce POR, and, only when necessary, modify it. One engineer observed, 'the whole virtual factory has to agree on [a change]. When something is POR it's impossible to change it.' During a period of cost consciousness, a proposal to revise a planned change at one fab was brought before a decision making body. Despite the appeal of cutting costs, the request was met with a barrage of criticism by the managers considering the proposal. 'I flat out don't support each factory coming in and saying they don't want to do things,' said one. 'That decision is POR and it can't be changed just because one fab objects to it,' added another.

Roadmaps, POR, and their production and perpetuation brought Moore's Law into the daily work of Chipco managers and engineers, guiding actions in the near term, and pacing change in the longer term.

The Here and Now

Every minute, or even second, seemed to count in making Moore's Law a reality. Tech engineers operated under an almost continual sense of crisis. Extending the logic that if 'there's no new process there's no Chipco,' managers and engineers were well aware of the value of a reliably working manufacturing process. 'Chipco has always been driven by time to market,' noted one manager, 'a month loss in time to market is worth [on the order of a billion dollars] in revenues.'

Because the manufacturing machine represented money, and the manufacturing machine under development represented future money, keeping it running at all times was critical. I was once in a training class when both of the instructors simultaneously checked the pagers on their belts, and bolted for the door. I was somewhat alarmed by their sudden, unexplained departure. As an occasional lunch-time jogger, I was well aware that running 'on campus' was a strict violation of Chipco safety rules. We were to walk to the edge of the property before picking up speed. About 20 minutes later our instructors returned to the class and apologized for their hasty departure. They explained that, as members of the ERT (Emergency

Response Team), they had responded to a call from the fab. Imagining a dire situation involving fire, chemicals or bodily harm, I was relieved to hear that nothing life-threatening had happened. The issue was nonetheless urgent. There had been a problem in the delivery of process control water to some of the fab tools. Had too many minutes gone by, tools may have been shut down or wafers lost. With four to six weeks of process time invested in each wafer, and completed wafers representing tens of thou-sands of dollars in potential revenue, any damage to wafers or tools was sorely felt. Even in Tech's development fab where the microprocessors made were rarely sold, the loss of wafers due to a mishap in the process opera-tion represented a loss of work and results, a cessation of action.

Summary: Time in Tech

For people engaged in technology development and manufacturing, time is a critical, limited, yet exploitable, resource. The focus on action, working to near term goals to develop new processes or working to keep a fab running at all times, draws attention to the rapid passage of time. But members of Tech and Manufacturing have the experience of being in control. The relentless pursuit and accomplishment of goals marks progress – once one set of goals is met, others are waiting. As each new manufacturing process generation was rolled out, another one was always in the making within Tech. On more than one occasion, people referred to the 'treadmill' of process development guided by Moore's Law, imply-ing linearity, predictability and unceasing progress. Indeed, the technical challenges of advancing on the treadmill were formidable, but overcom-ing them gave renewed confidence in progress. One Tech manager observed, 'I have heard my whole career that chips can't get faster than this, or smaller than that. At every turn in my career people have said there's a hard limit here and it hasn't turned out to be true. The slopes have gotten a little steeper [meaning the technical challenges have become greater] which means we have to put more people on the projects, or it might take a little longer.'

Past adherence to Moore's Law confirms the likelihood of future adher-ence; engineers have confidence in the unfolding of near future time as a result. The future exists not as a nebulous expanse but comes already carved into discrete units, unfolding as if governed by Moore's Law. Roadmaps are written using process generations as the scale, rather than years. While Moore's Law is the grandest pacing device that imposes routine on tech-nology development and manufacturing work, many other practices contribute to the pacing of time. Setting MBPs, writing weekly reports, attending daily fab meetings, and tracking ARs all serve to carve time into more fine-grained units and to anchor participants in the unfolding of time that accompanies the march of technology in this industry.

TECH CULTURE

The aspects of culture discussed in this chapter are summarized in Table 4.1. Through their work to improve chip manufacturing processes and their experimentation with and operation of the processes themselves, members of Tech experience the physical world as manipulable on a very fine scale and controllable within clearly defined boundaries. Their focused individual work and relatively limited interactions with others reflect the high degree of specialization and divisibility associated with the manufacturing processes themselves. Knowledge is gained through experimentation and data relied on to make decisions. Moore's Law paces the entire process development effort and renders particular aspects of it discrete.

Each aspect of the culture is strongly connected to the other aspects. The material aspects of chip manufacturing strongly shape the work practices within Tech, giving rise to the tight connections observed between cultural meanings. Moore's Law rests on the fundamental physical property of scalability – a region of any size can be electrically altered to make an electronic component of virtually any size on very high purity silicon wafers. The practical limit to scaling – the reduction in the physical size of the components on the chip – lies in the limits on the precision of the process technologies used.[5] Further, the depth, not just the area, of the silicon

Table 4.1   Key aspects of Tech culture

	Cultural understandings manifested in Tech work
Physical world	Precisely manipulable Boundaries are closely defined and maintained Controllable, replicable and divisible
Roles and interactions	Roles specialized around discrete modules, narrow work focus Interactions routinized and occur around specific goals, 'not FYI' Rules and criteria for success internally determined
Knowledge	Practical; aimed at results Gained through experimentation; communicated through data Enables control and replication
Time	Future time made discrete and paced by Moore's Law Limited, but exploitable, resource

altered can be precisely controlled, with material deposited or grown in layers as small as a few nanometers (one-billionth of a meter) on the wafer. This allows for the sequential assembly of a chip, layer by layer.

The material properties of scalability and divisibility support the role specialization and routinization of interaction observed. Scalability enables a pacing device like Moore's Law to be established and maintained, and lays out very clearly the technical progress that must be made from one process generation to the next. Its suggests that knowledge is gained linearly and predictably. And applying this knowledge to create the next generation of manufacturing process brings confidence in engineers' abilities to continue to manipulate matter at a small scale over time.

Reflecting on the work of Tech and Manufacturing, one manager noted that its 'like a big gyroscope, and the only thing you can do to change it is to give it new bearings.' Indeed, the frenzied activity around the center and the speed of this activity did seem, like a gyroscope, to give the entire process of developing and operating chip manufacturing processes an uncanny stability. Moore's Law gave it its current bearing, and understandings of the physical world, roles and interactions, knowledge, and time produced and reproduced through the work practices within Tech and Manufacturing maintained it on its course.

NOTES

1. Recall that all personal names are pseudonyms.
2. There have been many different versions of Moore's Law used in the years since Gordon Moore first made his prediction. Moore himself is purported to have said 'Moore's Law has been stated so many different ways one of them is bound to be right. I take credit for all of them.'
3. At the time of this study, the number of transistors on a chip was smaller.
4. Each manufacturing process generation is given a number.
5. There are also limits imposed by the fundamental physics of the electronic devices, and the capabilities of the materials. These limits have, in the past, driven improvements in process technologies or materials to overcome them.

5. Environmental work at Chipco

You can't push a rope

Tech manager on environmental issues

Roger, an EnviroTech manager[1], once filled me in on the history of Chipco's approach to environmental issues, and the events that led to the formation of his group. Earlier, he observed, environmental issues weren't ignored, but tended to be treated at the 'end of the pipe,' or once the manufacturing processes had been designed and installed. But over the preceding few years he added, 'we have done a lot to mainstream how we deal with environmental issues [to be more like] how we deal with other things.' As the company grew, environmental impacts began to be experienced as 'constraints,' whether through regulation, community reaction, or internal commitments – 'things we chose to do.' Roger had earlier noted that Chipco 'tends to focus on things that limit performance,' and he added 'when we recognized these things as constraints, we started to use the same business processes to manage them.'

How were environmental issues regarded at Chipco? What was the nature of the constraints they posed? And how were they approached with mainstream business processes? In this chapter I consider environmental work at Chipco, against a backdrop of the work of Tech and Manufacturing described in the previous chapter. I explore what constituted daily work for those involved in environmental work and from this again draw out cultural meanings associated with the physical world, individual roles and interactions, knowledge, and time to compare and contrast with those operating within Tech. While considerable effort was dedicated to the mainstreaming of environmental work, against norms of careful planning and measurement and the relentless pacing of technological innovation, considerable tensions also resulted. The physical world was less bounded, harder to manipulate, metrics were not universally agreed upon nor controlled internally, and a plethora of other actors had a say.

MAKING ENVIRONMENT FIT

One day in early summer I sat in the cafeteria at Chipco's Tech site with two EnviroTech managers, John and Harold. Both were in town for a face-to-face meeting of the environmental strategic decision making body the following day. On days like these, employees who worked together but were geographically dispersed spent much of their time in the cafeteria coalescing in small groups around a table, then dispersing and reforming in different combinations on the hour.

Harold informed John and me that he needed our help with something he had promised to do for his boss, the head of the Materials group. 'Materials needs a metric for its EH&S deliverables,' Harold said, referring to Environment, Health and Safety by its common acronym. John objected, noting that a single metric was misleading because environmental impacts varied so much by material. Furthermore, he added, sufficient data on EH&S properties are simply not available for most materials, and 'you need data to develop a metric.'

Harold countered that 'we have metrics for everything else, including things that have a hundred different definitions.' 'Take quality,' he continued, 'even though it depends so much on the material you are talking about, we still have come up with a simple metric for quality.' The issue, he said, is that 'EH&S is up there as an MBP[2] for Materials and if its there as an MBP we should be managing it. If we can't manage it and demonstrate it with a metric then people are going to ask why we have all these EH&S people in Materials if we can't even come up with a metric.'

John still regarded the quest for a single metric as 'shortsighted,' but added, 'that's how Chipco manages, we define a numeric metric and fix on it and work towards it.' Any metric would have to be very general so it could be feasibly measured, he noted. Harold suggested, 'something like "Materials introduces chemicals that are understood so that we can manage the EH&S impacts."' John thought for a moment and replied, 'well, maybe that's the metric.'

'What I threw out was a marshmallow,' admitted Harold, presumably implying the metric was rather squishy or ill-formed. 'Yep,' said John, 'but that's probably about as crisp as we can get right now.'

This interchange highlights tensions EnviroTech and others involved in environmental work at Chipco encountered daily. On the one hand, they were held to the same standards prevalent in Tech and Manufacturing and were expected to approach their work in a goal-oriented, results-focused way. On the other hand, the nature of the work was much less predictable, and certainly not driven by an overarching logic like Moore's Law. Lamenting that environmental management was often not seen as part of the pervasive 'safety culture' that was taken seriously by fab managers, senior management, and employees, one EH&S manager explained that safety issues were much easier to 'name.' 'It's very easy to say if a person cuts their finger that it's a safety incident, but with environment it's harder to say what counts; it's all in the eye of the beholder,' he explained. 'Some people believe that one molecule of a carcinogen poses a health risk, while others would do a risk assessment to weigh the risks against the benefits,' he added. Referring to Chipco's Corporate Strategic Objective to 'ensure a safe, clean, and injury-free workplace,' (known to most employees simply as 'Safety First') another manager claimed that one couldn't have the same goal for environment because 'everyone would be walking around saying "what am I supposed to be doing?"'

ENVIRONMENTAL WORK AND THE PHYSICAL WORLD: OUTSIDE THE FAB

What were those engaged in environmental work doing? What constituted action for these people, and what physical world did they engage? The action for the majority of environmental work at Chipco occurred outside the fab. It was not relegated to only one location though, with equipment and treatment systems often distributed around the clean room space on other floors of the building, in other buildings altogether, or even outside in the open. Some of the environmental treatment equipment, like scrubbers to clean air exhaust, were mounted on the roof of the fab building. Other equipment was housed in the basement of the fab building, or 'subfab.' Large tanks for neutralizing wastewater (called Acid Waste Neutralization, or AWN), sat outside the fab building. Across a paved parking area lay the CUB, or Central Utilities Building, a separate building that housed the equipment for power delivery and for making ultra-pure water (UPW) used in the fab.

Entering the subfab was considerably less burdensome than entering the fab. One simply opened the door and grabbed a hard hat and safety glasses from the rack on the wall. In the Tech subfab, many of the regulars were plumbers or electricians who were installing new equipment, or maintaining existing equipment. They simply kept their hard hats on at all times. And they dressed like plumbers and electricians – no bunny suits. In fact, the procedure seemed disarmingly simple in contrast to entering the fab, and it was typically not subject to the same level of public scrutiny. When I went through the subfab at one manufacturing site, Irene, the site EH&S engineer accompanying me saw that the rack for hard hats and safety glasses was empty. Three men walked past and she asked if they knew where the hard hats were, but they shrugged and continued into the subfab. Irene then cracked the door open to an adjacent room and asked the person there if she could borrow two sets from a stash lying on the floor, promising to return them. As an EH&S person, she confided, she felt she had to model the proper behavior.

Walking around the subfab one navigates aisles and aisles of equipment servicing the fab 'tools'[3] on the floor above. Pumps draw vacuums to pressurize chambers in the process tools, automated gas delivery systems send up the right amount of gas in the right mixtures to the appropriate tools, and POU or 'point of use' treatment systems remove or destroy pollutants from the effluent of a single tool. Overhead run pipes of all diameters and marked in all colors, to carry gases, chemical mixtures, water and air to the tools and back. With safety firmly in mind, gas lines are often triple contained, with several redundant automatic mechanisms (electrical and pressure actuated) for shutting off flow in case of a leak or emergency.

As Irene was showing me around the sub-fab, she pointed to a piece of equipment designed to remove organic chemicals from air emissions. Pleasantly surprised, Irene commented on how clean the equipment and ducting was, as it was usually coated with carbon dust that escaped from the carbon filter inside. A few months ago, she noted, the fab management started paying much more attention to the operation of the equipment. It had been hard to get technicians to take care of the equipment, but Irene's 'job got a whole lot easier' after she told fab management that properly taking care of the existing unit could save more than $1 million that would otherwise be needed to buy a second unit to meet air emissions targets.

A room near the main subfab was home to 'decon' (decontamination) and parts clean. Heavy duty rubber boots and face masks hung from the walls surrounding a central table and some cabinets. Here parts that were being shipped out of the fab were decontaminated 'even if it doesn't require it,' noted Irene. 'Even if something has water in it we won't ship it without draining it because other people handling it don't know what the liquid is,' she added. Parts clean was used to periodically clean parts from the fab tools. Before leaving the room Irene checked inside a large yellow storage cabinet to ensure all the chemicals inside were properly stored and labeled. Sometimes engineers have 'secret hiding places' for chemicals they don't tell EH&S about, she noted, but this time everything was in order.

The next room was entered through a roughly six-inch thick sliding metal door. Here hazardous waste from the process was stored before being shipped off site by a hazardous waste handler. Large square metal totes, roughly four feet on each side, and a number of metal drums captured and contained spent chemicals. Irene noted that 'there are so many rules' to do with hazardous waste. Totes and drums must be properly labeled, dated and stored a certain distance apart. The EH&S employee in charge of the hazardous waste program for the site was 'down a lot making sure the room is in order,' Irene noted. But, she added, the hardest thing about hazardous waste is 'explaining to [employees] what hazardous waste is because its not necessarily hazardous to you, there are various categories it falls into.'

Our final stop in the subfab was a room which housed prototype equipment to recycle a chemical mixture used in a critical process step. Here Irene had tried to line up another person in advance to show us around as she was not familiar with the equipment. But the 'room owner' was on vacation, so we stopped by to see who was on hand. Irene's badge did not allow her to swipe in but two engineers passing in the hall offered their badges, at the same time that a technician opened the room door to let us in. The engineers good naturedly told the technician, 'better watch out, she's a safety person.' Despite the fact that she managed the fab's air emissions programs, Irene's membership in the site's larger EH&S group no doubt associated her with the safety programs that were so vigilantly applied.

The technician offered to show us what he knew about the recycling equipment, which turned out to be quite a lot despite the fact that he was working only temporarily on it and described himself as 'a gas pad guy.' Two medium-sized white plastic tubs were at the center of the system, surrounded by plastic piping and a number of small pumps that automatically clicked on and off. One pipe came down through the ceiling from the fab, carrying used slurry (a solid/liquid mix) and emptied it into one tank. The technician indicated that when it reached two-thirds full, new slurry and then a 'replenisher' liquid was added. He pointed to a control monitor that showed a schematic of the system and a number of measurements, like pH and specific gravity in the tank. If the specifications of the recycled slurry batch were wrong, the technician noted, the system would automatically call for a 'POR mix,'[4] or new slurry drawn from a tote. Asked how the two slurries compared, he said that the recycled 'is better than the POR mix.' 'When they first switched over I heard it made yields better,' he added, 'so people were really happy.' Irene observed that this was a great 'win-win-win' on environmental impact, cost, and yield, especially after 'all the push-back' they'd experienced on it. The technician confirmed that it was working well, but added that he wasn't sure if other fabs would now adopt it because 'you know how they are about doing anything different.'

Summary: Environmental Work and the Physical World

For those engaged in environmental work, the physical world was only to a limited extent the world experienced by those in Tech – bounded, manipulable and controllable. The boundaries were neither physically nor procedurally as firmly established as those surrounding the fab. The subfab and other areas where emissions to the environment were captured, treated, or recycled were physically dispersed, and entered with varying degrees of procedural formality. The need for boundary control was much lower. Whereas cleanliness and careful control of the physical environment was an essential prerequisite to work within the fab, environmental work was somewhat more forgiving. The carbon dust Irene referred to represented little more than a sign of inefficiency in the equipment, and one that had persisted for several years; it did not grind the operation to a halt.

Nonetheless, boundaries were important and flows of materials from inside Chipco to the outside were salient to some employees, as Irene's awareness of the treatment of decontaminated parts and hazardous waste suggested. Indeed, one site EH&S manager said he visualized his 'campus' (the site of the fab plus its supporting buildings and co-located office buildings) as 'a bubble with a bottom.' His role was 'knowing everything that goes on inside and what materials cross the boundary between inside and outside.'

This knowledge of material flows, however, surely gave little more than an illusion of control to those engaged in environmental work. Complex rules and regulations, set by outsiders, governed what constituted waste and frequently influenced how it was to be treated. And internally, the environmental engineer faced a physical reality that was handed to her by Tech and Manufacturing. Rarely could an environmental engineer influence process conditions – concentrations or constituents of waste – to optimize environmental treatment conditions.[5] Even when process performance improved, as it did with the recycled slurry, the conservatism associated with operating a working manufacturing process suppressed the scope for change. One Tech engineer who was sympathetic to environmental issues observed that 'we can't just change the solids in the effluent from 30 percent to 20 percent just to satisfy [Mark Smith]' (an environmental engineer working on a waste treatment system for a new manufacturing process). A Tech manager, also sympathetic to such issues and dedicated to improving the design of environmentally preferable manufacturing technologies argued that the environmental design would always lag process decisions somewhat, saying 'you can't push a rope.' 'We all know the real lead is going to be the [process] technology, rather than environmental things,' she added.

Equally important to how the physical world showed up in environmental work – as weakly bounded, and controlled and manipulated according to others' rules – is how the physical world did *not* show up in environmental work. Perhaps naively, I expected I might hear references to the 'outside' – the ecosystem and natural environment. But there was an almost complete silence on such issues. Only once in nine months of observation did I hear a biological species mentioned, when an EH&S employee presented modeling results and discussed discharge limits on copper in wastewater in terms of the sensitivity of trout. On this and one other occasion, a particular river was named. Much more frequently, discharge or emissions limits were stated only as a numerical concentration, or as numerical targets established by regulation or internal consensus. This reduced the complexity of what was really outside, and rendered it manageable. On one occasion, an EnviroTech manager was presenting a plan to 'minimize adverse global climate change impacts' when a senior manager present objected to the wording. It was much too broad, he argued and could imply a huge range of actions, including that Chipco would build all its fabs 'above the high water mark.' The presenter explained that the plan really referred to the 'regulatory issues and the impacts on our business.' Change the wording, then, the senior manager suggested, because 'we're not trying to solve world hunger here.' Such choices are more than simply linguistic; they shape what problems are attended to and delineate the slice of the natural, physical world that is admitted for consideration.

ROLES AND INTERACTIONS FOR ENVIRONMENTAL WORK: ORDERING THE OUTSIDE

Just as environmental work was largely separated physically from the fab, those who did it also had limited interaction with members of Tech or Manufacturing. In fact, those who routinely work in the subfab rarely, if ever, go into the fab. I was shocked when a 20-year veteran who worked as a subfab electrician asked the instructor at a training class what the ultra-pure water was used for once it got to the fab. One of the most essential and basic materials used in the fab, ultra-pure water is used whenever water will touch the wafers, such as during rinse steps, and whenever water will touch process equipment that will then touch the wafers. Indeed, the training class in which this question was asked was designed explicitly to introduce those who worked in manufacturing support roles – such as in the subfab and servicing factory systems like the air handling, electrical and gas delivery systems – to how these systems impacted fab equipment, and how they could be serviced safely and with minimal disruption to the fab. The goal was to 'show people that all the different pieces fit together to make a fab fit together.' The instructors shared some cautionary tales, emphasizing that safety and continued fab operation were never to be compromised. In one case, a custodian had plugged in a vacuum cleaner and tripped a breaker for power to a monitoring system, making it appear as if the ultra-pure water system had gone down and 'sending everyone scrambling.' In another case, an instructor warned that working on a scrubber that removes air emissions from the fab could trigger an automatic evacuation if the air flow is not compensated for, and that 'you don't want to end up with all the bunny suits in the parking lot unnecessarily.'

Engineers and managers who worked on the design and development of environmental treatment equipment were generally more aware of fab operations, but rarely had direct experience working within the fab. One Tech engineer was dedicated to providing this experience for a Facilities engineer with whom he worked closely on the development of an environmental treatment system. Ideally, the Tech engineer noted, Facilities engineers should be trained as if they were a fab engineer, and they should even 'run some WIP (work in progress).'[6] 'It sucks but it would be a great way of learning,' he added, referring to the intensity and arduous hours that characterize the initiation of a new Tech engineer.

The organization of environmental work, however, had not historically followed the 'boot camp' model in Tech where new engineers were assigned as 'tool owners' on older pieces of process equipment and initiated by learning how to operate these tools – typically round the clock – in a high pressure development or manufacturing environment. Environmental work not only was formally organized across numerous diverse and geographically dispersed groups, but it also had historically drawn in people with varying experience and expertise. Table 5.1 summarizes the key groups involved in environmental work at Chipco at the time of this study.

Because of the number of groups involved, their different foci and reporting structures, and the nature of the work itself, interaction between those engaged in environmental work was much less routinized than it was within Tech and manufacturing. The design, installation, and operation of environmental treatment systems, like air exhaust scrubbers or wastewater treatment systems, was historically separate from the tasks associated with compliance with environmental regulation or the initiation of new environmental management approaches. The former was typically done by facilities engineers and technicians and the latter by site and/or corporate environmental specialists, as part of the Environment, Health and Safety (EH&S) group. While facilities engineers and site EH&S specialists typically both reported to site management, they did not generally report to the site's fab management. Instead, they reported in to managers in fab support roles who also oversaw everything from janitorial work and operating the cafeteria to providing the infrastructure for delivering water, gas and energy to the fabs.

Site environmental engineers tended to divide up the work according to major categories of waste and the regulations that govern them. For example, at Irene's manufacturing site, one environmental engineer 'owned' the hazardous waste management program, she owned air emissions and a third engineer owned wastewater. (At a larger fab there might be as many at ten site environmental engineers, who would share responsibility for programs.) In practice, role delineations in site EH&S groups were somewhat more

Table 5.1   *Formal organization of environmental work at Chipco*

Group Name	Description/Role
Site Environment, Health and Safety (EH&S)	• Ensure environmental treatment equipment is operating appropriately and achieving regulatory requirements • Plan for installation of new treatment equipment • Track data for regulatory compliance and report to regulatory authorities
Corporate Environment, Health and Safety (EH&S)	• Monitor regulatory and other developments that influence corporate-wide environmental approaches • Negotiate with industry members and regulatory agencies regarding approaches for emerging environmental issues • Manage and coordinate existing site environmental programs and ensure overall regulatory compliance
EnviroTech	• Anticipate needs and develop solutions for environmentally preferable manufacturing processes for process generation under development • Interface with Tech to develop and deliver environmental treatment solutions along with new manufacturing processes
Facilities Environmental	• Assist in the development and operation of environmental treatment equipment
Materials	• Select and obtain all of the materials – gases, chemicals, and other consumables – used in the fab • Consider environmental impact among selection criteria

Note: Group names, with the exception of Site and Corporate Environment, Health, and Safety, are pseudonyms.

flexible than those in Tech. Irene knew broadly what her colleagues were working on, even though she was not an expert on their equipment or regulations. Similarly, outsiders saw them as less specialized – indeed, being mistaken for and labeled a 'safety person' was not an isolated incident, and one that other site EH&S employees complained about with some regularity.

The corporate EH&S group supported the work of site EH&S employees, but was itself diverse. Several hundred specialists, ranging from industrial hygienists to nurses, ergonomics specialists and environmental engineers, were employed by this group. Many were located at one geographical site, co-located with a large manufacturing fab. But a large number of corporate EH&S employees were also located at manufacturing or non-manufacturing sites around the world. The environmental engineers and managers in the

corporate group monitored and prepared for emerging regulatory requirements and generated overall policy for Chipco's regulatory and voluntary
environmental approaches. They coordinated with the site EH&S groups,
but were not directly involved in their day-to-day management.

New Roles

Despite the significant number and variety of people doing environmentally related work at Chipco, there had not been a group dedicated to
the development of environmental approaches for future manufacturing
processes until a few years before my study. The first step toward such a
group was taken about five years prior to my participant observation when
a high-level decision-making body, the Strategic Environmental Policy
Council (SEPC, a pseudonym), was created to ensure the availability
of new chemicals and new process approaches critical to Chipco's future
manufacturing processes. The SEPC adopted proactive environmental
policies, such as the pollution prevention hierarchy,[7] but had little direct
influence over individual process development projects. The SEPC was dis-
solved a few years later, with the intention that emerging environmental
issues be addressed at a more tactical level, closer to the core activities of
Tech. Two changes were made within the year.

First, a new group, EnviroTech, the group in which I participated, was
formally created to work with Tech to develop environmentally preferable
manufacturing processes at the design stage. Many of EnviroTech's three
managers and eight engineers had been working in this capacity informally
for several years already, but they brought together quite different backgrounds. One manager had worked in the corporate EH&S group, one in the
Facilities and Construction group, and the third within the Manufacturing
group. The three managers, and the engineers who worked for them, were
distributed among three primary geographic locations; none of the managers were co-located. Furthermore, none of the managers were located at
the Tech site where the primary development fab was located. Although
members of the group traveled extensively, much of their interaction was by
email or through telephone conferences.

Whereas environmental engineers tended to specialize by media (emissions to air, water, or land), and Tech engineers specialized by process type
and chip layer, the members of EnviroTech had somewhat more fluid roles,
taking on issues as they came up and perhaps managing different aspects
of them according to their expertise. For example, the former corporate
EH&S manager worked on issues that needed a lot of liaison with others
in the industry or with regulatory authorities. But the former Facilities and
Construction manager worked on related aspects of the same issues.

Furthermore, each member of EnviroTech simultaneously worked on a number of projects which were not necessarily related to each other. Finally, largely for historical reasons, the group resided in the larger Materials organization, which supported Tech and Manufacturing but was a separate group with separate management. Commenting on the limitations of this arrangement, one member noted, 'there are a lot of synergies around environmental issues across the organization, and a lot of them are non-materials issues.' Nonetheless, the group remained where it was.

A second formal change accompanying the formation of EnviroTech was the creation of the EnviroCouncil, modeled upon the standard and successful TechCouncils. The EnviroCouncil met monthly and was comprised of members from Tech, Facilities, Manufacturing, Equipment, Materials, the Corporate EH&S group, and the newly created EnviroTech group. The EnviroCouncil tracked environmental process development projects, determining which projects to undertake, interfacing with appropriate TechCouncils to understand relevant process developments and to lobby for the environmental projects, and reviewing data and recommendations brought by project teams to make and formally ratify project decisions (for example, equipment selections).

Coordination of Environmental Work

Work in Tech was coordinated by setting and measuring progress toward specific module target specifications and other easily shared metrics. Such metrics were harder to come by for environmental work as developments were not driven by an overarching logic like Moore's Law. Nonetheless, many, like the Materials manager in the opening vignette in this chapter, sought them. Indeed, one Tech engineer who had worked intensively on improving an environmental treatment system told me that to get Tech to pay attention to environmental issues one had to develop a very simple environmental goal for each process module. He suggested using 'a binary system, where you would score a 1 if you did the environmentally correct thing and a 0 if you didn't.' But as John, an EnviroTech manager, noted in his objection to the proposed MBP, 'there is no way that something like a [complex environmental planning] activity could be incorporated [into a single metric].' 'The problem with this is that it narrows your thinking,' he added.

Much thinking continued about how to set and communicate environmental goals. The EnviroCouncil had taken on the roadmapping process prevalent in Tech as a way of representing and generating agreement on environmental performance parameters for future process modules, and specifying environmental treatment plans. Their deliberate but slightly confused discussion of various roadmaps at one EnviroCouncil meeting demonstrates the importance placed on mastering the process of roadmapping and consequently establishing metrics for environmental aspects of process development. Almost 40 minutes into the meeting, the time allotted on the agenda to 'roadmap review' had long since come and gone. People were still engaged in discussion of three different but related environmental roadmaps that had been presented. Dave, a roadmap owner and site environmental engineer expressed reservations that items on his roadmap were outside his realm of authority. '[Am I] the right owner of this roadmap given that there are processes on here that the fab isn't doing yet?' he asked. Jack, a Facilities manager, sought further clarification, 'Is the purpose of this to look at future plans overall or to track how the fabs differ from each other?' Rick, the EnviroCouncil chair, tried to clarify the intention of roadmapping. 'We're trying to emulate the roadmap process of the TechCouncils,' he noted, adding, 'if you look at the TechCouncil roadmaps they have a lot of information, including things like metrology, external research, etc. We need something that captures all of the environmental issues. Maybe there's a way to combine the Facilities roadmap and Dave's roadmap.'

A discussion ensued about how the roadmaps would reflect existing and planned procedures and equipment, how exceptions and changes would be handled, and the role of the EnviroCouncil and other management bodies in handling them. 'Can Rick document this in the minutes?' asked Jack, 'because there is a lot of confusion.' Rick agreed and described the kind of roadmaps he wanted the group to work toward. A detailed roadmap should be created that included environmental treatment specifications for all of the process equipment, but there would also be a high-level roadmap of the numerical environmental goals for Chipco as a whole. Rick remarked that 'We've generated more ARs (Action Required) than ever before in a roadmap discussion, but it's a good thing because of the level of confusion of who's doing what.'

Even with this attention to coordination and clarification of roles and work through roadmapping, unknowns persisted. At one presentation of environmental roadmap goals for a new process under development, several people commented on the fact that the row in the table for energy consumption was blank. One manager joked that this must mean that the engineer in charge of quantifying Chipco's energy consumption was going to 'convert all the factories to cold fusion.' The presenter noted that a goal would be added, but that accurately quantifying existing energy consumption was difficult and time-consuming, and this needed to be done before reasonable projections and goals could be set.

Even in cases where goals existed and could be shared, they were not necessarily widely known or acted upon. One Tech employee who had a personal interest in environmental issues reported he was surprised to hear a Tech manager mention an environmental emissions goal in a selection meeting for a new type of process tool. Normally, he noted, 'the selection criteria are cost, run rate, and reliability.' For a different process tool an EH&S engineer reported to the EnviroCouncil that particular environmental goals were not being worked on by the team responsible for the new tool selection. 'Were the teams pushing back on the environmental goals?' he was asked. 'No, the problem was that they actually didn't know they had to meet them and they hadn't started gathering the necessary data [from the supplier],' the EH&S engineer answered, admitting, 'we need to do more work to educate them on the environmental issues.'

Summary: Roles and Interactions for Environmental Work

Environmental work at Chipco was formally organized across a range of groups, and performed by a large number of people. While the traditional work of designing and operating environmental treatment systems and complying with regulatory standards was often segregated by media – emissions to air, water, or land – roles were not nearly as distinct as those within Tech. Efforts were increasingly made to address environmental issues holistically, but such efforts were complex and often unpredictable. Choices about possible environmental approaches were shaped by details of the manufacturing process that were largely predetermined. And choices were further constrained by external actors – regulators, communities and others – and subject to change with changes in scientific understanding, political actions or public opinion. Further, by virtue of their diverse backgrounds and positions within other groups, those doing environmental work typically did not enjoy the status of those who were closely associated with developing or operating a manufacturing fab. One Tech manager remarked that an environmental engineer working on a model of chemical use in the fab would not be able to judge the validity of the results because 'he's never even been inside a fab.' The physical separation of the work space was mirrored in the formal and informal divisions between those engaged in process related and environmental work.

Finally, the metrics and goals used to coordinate work within the community of environmental specialists, and especially between this community and Tech, were not yet well established, nor did it appear that they could ever be as established as they were in Tech. The physical property of scalability in the production of chips, and the logic of Moore's Law that reflected this scalability and generated the expectation of its continued achievement gave Tech the ability to set discrete and detailed criteria for success (module target specifications). Furthermore, the capacity to achieve these goals was largely internally determined. This predictability led to highly specialized roles and highly routinized interactions, characteristic of 'insulated' social interaction. Those doing environmental work did not experience the same level of insulation, though they strove to emulate Tech's roadmapping and goal setting practices. Their transactions with each other, with Tech, and with outsiders remained broader and more negotiable, partly due to the stage they were at in measuring environmental performance and setting goals and partly due to the uncertain and distributed nature of knowledge production and consumption about environmental effects.

ENVIRONMENTAL WORK AND KNOWLEDGE: WORKING ON ENVIRONMENTAL ORDER

Work in Tech was oriented toward solving specific technical problems on an aggressive schedule to contribute to practical, working process modules. The focus and discipline displayed by Tech engineers was enabled in part due to broad agreement on the nature of the problems to be solved. Moore's Law provided the overarching end for their efforts, and individual process module specifications were generated to meet this end. The problems for environmental work were neither as clear nor as easily agreed upon. Indeed, they often were not easy to map out in advance. One Tech manager expressed her exasperation with a particular environmental issue that affected her process modules by complaining that the issue had 'just came from somewhere.' It hadn't been on any of the roadmaps, and she blamed EnviroTech for this. This particular issue, which involved a newly identified greenhouse gas, was still uncertain in scientific circles and had only recently come to the attention of the semiconductor manufacturing industry as a whole.

Several months into my stay at Chipco, I became involved in a small way with a task force that had been set up to consider how Chipco evaluated the environmental and labor practices of its overseas suppliers of materials and components. After sitting through several seemingly interminable two-hour teleconferences on this subject, with the conversation cycling endlessly around topics of what supplier audits were currently done; who did them; which suppliers one should audit for environmental and labor practices; how one identified these suppliers; how one trained the people currently doing supplier audits to add new items to their audit; how one modified the training programs given that they were all in the process of modification for other reasons anyway; how one would pilot the evaluations and pilot the training of the evaluators, and so on. One member of the task force expressed concern about the lack of action, or even a plan for action. The member suggested that, 'part of the problem is that people don't know what problem we have to solve, so they're not energized to solve the problem.'

For this and many other environmentally-related issues, problems were not clearly delineated with numeric targets and prescribed timetables derived from a single governing logic, like Moore's Law. Their solutions did not necessarily need to coincide with the cycle of new process development, and, importantly, the quality of the solution was not largely determined internally. Despite this, EnviroTech and others engaged in environmental work sought to mimic the data-based decision processes so prevalent within Tech.

Just the Facts . . .

To gain approval to operate the slurry recycling system I had seen with Irene, extensive data had been collected to demonstrate that it did not adversely affect process quality or yield, 12 revisions of a 'white paper' had been written, and the white paper had been reviewed by ten decision-making bodies. For this and other projects, those doing environmental work increasingly realized that they needed to portray their arguments through hard data, where possible. One EH&S manager had been put in charge of developing an environmental decision support tool for the EnviroCouncil. The manager prepared a series of questions in different categories that were designed to elicit the 'facts and data' needed to make a decision. It contained several categories, like 'employee and community perception and comfort,' that were regarded as highly subjective by some EnviroCouncil members. One manager was uncomfortable sharing the method with Tech because it looked 'too subjective' for their tastes. 'They make decisions using different priorities from those EH&S uses to make decisions,' he suggested.

The manager developing the decision support tool emphasized that 'the tool does not make the decision, it tells you what facts and data are needed to make the decision.' But discussion continued in this and a subsequent EnviroCouncil meeting about the design of the tool and its potential for acceptance. At one point as the group was reviewing items within each category one concerned member asked, 'how measurable are these things?' Another questioned whether the decision tool was 'really a way to cost justify doing environmental projects,' in which case, he argued, it ought to include cost. Eventually, in response to a question from the EnviroCouncil chair on whether the 'right mix of objective and subjective questions' were included in the tool, most members agreed that it should be adopted.

The uneasiness about the environmental decision support tool reflects a broader tension between the desire of those doing environmental work to have it accepted as data driven and hence legitimate to Tech, and a recognition – at least by many of them – that environmental problems often could not be adequately represented only by 'facts and data.' Nonetheless, there was a certain confidence that data based decisions would prevail. The same EH&S manager who was in charge of developing the environmental decision support tool was discussing the Natural Step program with me. This external program aims to help companies evaluate their environmental impact by assessing how they stand on four simple 'system conditions,' like 'substances produced by society must not systematically increase in nature', and 'substances from the earth's crust must not systematically increase in nature.' The manager felt that the Natural Step was based on reasonable principles, but suggested that they were too simplistic and not 'data driven' enough for Chipco. The problem, he noted, was that the principles talked about thermodynamics, but not about kinetics – 'we all know the world is going to end,' he added, 'the question is when.'

Others emphasized the importance of data in the portrayal of Chipco's environmental actions to the outside world. Generally reticent to sign up to outsiders' programs, Chipco continually urged others to 'judge us by our results.' Commenting on the value of obtaining certification to an externally developed environmental management system that some companies were adopting, one EH&S manager suggested that for Chipco it would 'go backwards; it would lower the bar.' On another occasion during an EnviroCouncil discussion on the details of a proposed new public commitment on greenhouse gas emissions, one manager observed 'We're very careful about the results we go after because we're going to get the results, so we'd better be specific about what we want.' A second manager, added 'If we don't have the facts and solutions we won't commit.'

One member asked how a change in the technical approach for capturing one class of chemicals would influence the internal goal of reducing these chemical emissions per wafer for each subsequent manufacturing process. The comment was dismissed by someone who remarked that as long as the ultimate goal was met over several years' time, that was what mattered. Internal goals were important, however, to 'make sure we have the right milestones . . . so we understand where we're going and that we're making progress on it,' he later added.

. . . And Opinions

Despite the importance of facts, the desire to muster them and effort to do so, opinions mattered. The opinions of outside community members, of regulatory agencies, and of scientists were important and shaped choices and actions taken on environmental issues. Some of these opinions were holdovers from earlier concerns, but they nonetheless were important to ongoing decisions.

For example, the 'environmental' concern most well-known to those not directly engaged in environmental work was Chipco's restriction on the use of odorous chemicals. Following community concern over an odorous chemical that resulted in costly and disruptive last-minute changes in the construction of a new fab, engineers in other locations were reticent to introduce new chemicals with strong odors. One Materials engineer had rejected several options for use in a process step because of their odor. She explained that this decision was often very difficult for chemical suppliers to understand, especially when the chemicals were environmentally benign. The engineer hired a consultant to measure threshold values, or the limit of detectability of the chemical by the human nose, for one of the chemicals.[8] Armed with these data she sought approval from multiple decision-making bodies, and finally brought the decision before the EnviroCouncil. Rather than give a firm answer, the EnviroCouncil neither condemned nor approved the chemical. In the end, the chemical was not chosen – bringing a smelly new chemical in to use at Chipco was simply considered too risky.

A second area where the opinion of communities mattered greatly was in the use of water. EnviroTech managers were very surprised when a senior executive responded to their newly prepared strategic long range plan by stating that more attention was needed to water consumption by the fabs, and to developing manufacturing processes that would conserve or reuse water. After carefully documenting air emissions issues and giving them the greatest attention in the plan, the EnviroTech managers were somewhat taken aback. While air emissions were the 'number one problem' for environmental management, water consumption was the 'number one gap,' they rationalized. One observed that the executive 'had his growth hat on.' '[The executive's] perspective is on growth and water supply limits it,' he added. Others who had been involved in environmental work for a long time recognized that Chipco's use of water was lower than that of many industries, but also knew it was a public image issue that the industry would be dealing with for a long time. One manager noted, shaking his head, 'we're tagged as water hogs and we can't shake that image.' EnviroTech set about preparing a new 'water roadmap' immediately.

In matters of environmental regulation problems were not clearly defined either, and were similarly subject to the opinions of outsiders and insiders. The EnviroCouncil grappled for some time with an air emission for which the regulation was characterized as 'clearly ambiguous' by a Corporate EH&S manager. A visible but environmentally harmless plume was emitted sporadically from the fabs, and was more noticeable on clear dry days than on rainy ones. While the constituents of the plume were not regulated, the plume itself could qualify as a visual nuisance to the surrounding community. Reviewing the relevant regulation on nuisances and other emissions, the EH&S manager observed that Chipco could get 'pushed on one of these regulatory gray areas' if it left the plumes untreated. What made the decision to ultimately adopt treatment difficult was reluctance by some members of the EnviroCouncil to see the community concern as 'data.' Further, only certain communities – those in arid climates – tended to notice the plumes and periodically inquire about them while those in wet climates registered no concern.

Site-specific differences and regional variation were hard to square with Chipco's strong preference for identical replication across all fabs. During a period of heavy rain an EH&S engineer complained about the leaking roof of his small building that was adjacent to the main fab and office buildings. He shrugged, resigned to the plunk of rain dropping into buckets near his desk, and noted that the design of the flat roofed building had been replicated based on one in Arizona. Site specific differences also mattered for regulatory limits. An EnviroTech engineer once asked why regulatory limits for a certain set of chemicals appeared so 'arbitrary' across Chipco locations. One of the EH&S staff explained that these limits were set for regions based on the quality of the air, and many factors including population density, industrial activity and climate came into determining the limit for a given region. She added that the limits were expected to change, in response to changes in the different regions' air quality. 'Why can't Chipco just fight these changes?' the EnviroTech engineer questioned, implying that a uniform approach for all fabs, like Tech's, was far more desirable.

Scientific uncertainty further compounded regulatory ambiguity. The high global warming potential[9] and extremely long atmospheric lifetimes of a class of gases used by the semiconductor industry had attracted attention several years before my study.[10] Suppliers of the gases and regulatory agencies sought to control emissions of the gases to the atmosphere. Several people working on the issue within Chipco remained unconvinced by the science on global climate change, but acknowledged that it would be prudent to act and reduce emissions. One, noting the very long atmospheric lifetimes of the gases asked 'can you guarantee that they're going to be OK for 50 000 years?' Another noted that reducing the emissions was the 'right thing to do because it doesn't make sense to be using chemicals that have thousand-year atmospheric lifetimes, whether global warming is happening or not, which, by the way, I'm not sure its happening, but there's enough science that it's a potential issue.' Of course, even the atmospheric lifetime of some of these gases was still a subject of debate in the scientific community, which prompted one manager to remark that evaluating the global warming potential of these gases was 'a political science, not an exact science.'

Regulatory and other demands were not infrequently classed as 'political' by those working on them. A Facilities engineer made the following distinction: 'If EPA sets a limit and their data look reasonable, then we have to work on it, but in other areas the limits are more political and the data is conflicting.' Indeed, 'political' was a label used to contrast with the ideal of 'data driven.'

Operating 'In a Box'

Tradeoffs were another constant experienced by those doing environmental work at Chipco. Even in cases where problems were clearly delineated, data unequivocal, and limits clearly set, the nature of the work and the constraints imposed by the semiconductor manufacturing process often made optimal solutions very difficult to attain. Despite their desire to ultimately reduce emissions of harmful chemicals as much as possible, many of those working on environmental issues recognized the inherent limitations. Rarely was it straightforward to fully destroy the complex chemicals used in the manufacturing process, or to render them completely environmentally benign. Often treatment methods transformed chemicals into another chemical form, or shifted the medium in which they appeared, say from air to water. An EnviroTech engineer working on a system to remove fluorinated chemicals from air emissions noted that:

> Because you need [fluorine] to clean [compound S, necessary in the manufacturing process], you are operating within a box; with [fluorine] you are either going to get lots of HAPs [Hazardous Air Pollutants][11] and a little [greenhouse gases], or lots of [greenhouse gases] and a few HAPs – [the fluorine] has to come out one way or another.

At other times, primary environmental treatment to remove or destroy a certain chemical produced secondary environmental impacts, like increased energy or water consumption. Explaining why Chipco rejected an early proposal, popular with other industry members, for combusting excess greenhouse gases, an EnviroTech manager noted that 'abatement would have increased NOx emissions[12] and increased water usage [at one site] by 50 percent.' He added, 'It's not too difficult to destroy [the chemicals] at high concentrations [by combustion], but the gas stream for Chipco is very dilute.' A dilute gas stream implied that a great deal of air would need to be heated as well as the constituent chemicals, further increasing the amount of energy and water used for combustion.

Further contributing to insiders' impressions that environmental treatment was an inexact science was the fact that categorical answers on the treatment of a given emission were not always possible. Tech engineers approached an EH&S manager for advice on how to deal with the wastewater generated by a process step that used a mixture of water and a relatively benign chemical, isopropyl alcohol. The answer, the EH&S manager suggested, depended on the mixture they were using. If they used greater than a certain percentage of alcohol, the waste would be collected and sent to a third party for recycling, and if they used less than a much smaller percentage, the waste could go down the drain with other industrial wastewater. If they used a percentage somewhere in between, treating the waste would be very cumbersome.

A final source of tradeoffs that influenced environmental work came from its interaction with issues of safety. Chipco had long had an extremely active focus on safety, and a trip to somewhere as seemingly benign as the cafeteria could confirm this. Large poster board signs were positioned right beside the cashiers to remind people that 'all beverage containers MUST have lids.' A clown's face and the words 'We are NOT joking around' were included for extra encouragement. Following remodeling of the cafeteria serving areas, signs next to the soup tureens explained the proper way to ladle soup. Holding the bowl with one hand and ladling with the other was considered too dangerous because, the sign noted, all soups were kept at 165°F (74°C). Even crossing the paved walkway between two adjacent buildings could be considered hazardous in adverse weather. A stocked umbrella stand at one end of the walkway was marked 'For use on the walkway only. Please use safely.'

These directives might seem paternalistic, but were consistent with the safety philosophy at Chipco. Behavioral expectations inside the fab were even more stringent. Tech engineers were well aware of the emphasis on 'safety first,' above all else. One engineer in a training class offered that safety was a 'key assumption' of Tech's culture, calling it 'life before line yield.' 'But not before die yield,' joked the instructor. (Line yield is productivity metric for the overall manufacturing line, measured as the percentage of wafers started that are properly completed; die yield is the percentage of chips that are defect-free.) The first item on the agenda of quarterly Corporate EH&S update meetings was always a report on the safety statistics from Chipco's sites worldwide. Discussion of incidents (of which there were very few), trends (which were hard to discern with so few incidents in the sample), and new safety initiatives could easily take a half hour or more of meeting time. Tech BUMs and other staff meetings often included a safety review as one of the first items on the agenda.

The emphasis on safety had resulted, over time, in some flammable or unstable gases and chemicals being replaced by more stable variants as they became available. But several of these safe, stable materials posed environmental challenges for the very same reasons they were considered safe. Their stability meant they degraded only very slowly, or not at all, in the natural environment, or that they needed aggressive treatment to be broken down into more benign constituents. One manager observed that the 'reason we use [a class of greenhouse gases] is because they are safe, but in some people's minds we're polluting the environment.' A much earlier effort replaced an ozone depleting chemical which had been used because it was a safe form for the delivery of chlorine to process steps. In that case, an environmentally superior gas was rejected because it was corrosive and unsafe, and a new liquid chlorine source that offered good safety and environmental performance was adopted. The Manufacturing engineer who chaired the team responsible for finding the alternative recalled their selection criteria. The material, he noted, needed to be 'safe, non-toxic, ozone-friendly, manufacturable, and cost-effective.'

Summary: Environmental Work and Knowledge

With all these criteria, the lack of predictability, and the tradeoffs associated with safety and environmental impact, the 'box' in which environmental specialists worked was often quite limited. Further, these uncertainties and dependencies meant that the Tech engineer's dream of a 'binary' system for environmentally 'good' or 'bad' approaches was unrealistic at best. In contrast to the practical, replicable and internally controllable knowledge that members of Tech produced and consumed, environmental knowledge was much messier. Problems were highly contingent on chemical forms and concentrations, emissions media, regulatory limits, site-specific differences and, at least sometimes, outsiders' perceptions. While they recognized these as limitations on their ability to propose 'data driven' solutions, those engaged in environmental work also sought to use practices prevalent in Tech – like setting roadmap goals and gathering 'facts and data' – to anticipate and represent environmental problems and solutions.

Different employees had different mechanisms for coping with this tension. One manager noted for his wry sense of humor came up with his own metric for greenhouse gas emissions. He considered the standard units – million metric tonnes carbon equivalents (MMTCE) – cumbersome and nonintuitive, so in one presentation converted MMTCE into the equivalent amount of methane produced by feedlot cattle and dubbed it 'bull years,' revealing at the same time his personal opinions on the state of the science on global climate change. Others, like the one who fought the development of a single EH&S metric in the opening vignette in this chapter, openly struggled with the challenges of representing environmental knowledge and its implications. One EH&S manager explained that environmental issues are not 'monolithic' and 'there is no silver bullet checklist that [Chipco] can use.' 'In my honest opinion, what is needed is a better relationship and earlier involvement of EH&S in [Tech] activities,' he added. The problem with 'silver bullet' approaches is that you end up 'always trying to solve yesterday's problem . . . you are not dealing with today's issues which might be quite different.'

ENVIRONMENTAL WORK AND TIME: PLANNING, ADJUSTING, AND REACTING

Silver bullets aside, EnviroTech and others involved in environmental work were always seeking improved ways to anticipate and plan for new environmental challenges associated with the manufacturing process. The overarching logic of roadmapping – establishing detailed trajectories for process equipment, and performance parameters, all paced by expected adherence to Moore's Law – pervaded much activity throughout Chipco, and environmental work was no exception. Specific environmental goals for processes, or entire fabs where these were more relevant, had begun to be set several years before my study. These goals were represented on several related roadmaps, some of which were owned by EnviroTech and others owned by fab environmental engineers. While the roadmapping process reflected an assumption that processes, parameters and goals would change on a relatively predictable two-year cycle, such an assumption was only partly appropriate for the pacing of environmental work.

Indeed, some environmental projects relied heavily on the type of chemicals or gases used and when these changed with a new process generation, changes in environmental treatment were sometimes necessary. In these cases, roadmapping was helpful but roadmap parameters were hard to define closely as they depended so heavily on Tech's roadmaps. As the Tech manager had observed, 'you can't push a rope' and often chemical compositions, forms, and concentrations were not finalized until relatively late in the process development cycle. An EnviroTech engineer reflected this constraint when he noted that 'we don't even have [a plan for equipment]' for the next generation manufacturing process, beyond the one currently in development. 'Until we have that we won't know the chemistries and gases so we can't design any systems,' he added.

This same engineer was involved in a major development effort for a system that would capture greenhouse gases for subsequent recycling. For nearly three years, engineers had been working to develop and operate a pilot system that had been held back by numerous unanticipated technical glitches. It now looked likely that the manufacturing process generation (and associated gases) for which the system was designed and optimized would be on its way out before the capture units were ready. Many supported continuing the development of the systems and implementing them anyway, while others questioned how necessary they were. A voluntary agreement bound Chipco and others in the industry to reduce emissions of these gases, but there were other possible ways to treat them, and the voluntary agreement existed in the absence of regulatory limits. One EnviroTech engineer wondered aloud at an EnviroCouncil meeting, 'How long will it take the government to get regulation on this, ten years at least, and by then everything will be using [a new chemical] and it won't matter.' Environmental roadmapping was subject to the expectations and actions generated by Moore's Law, but not in any way that gave those doing it much sense of control over actual outcomes.

Other environmental problems invoked larger scale factory systems, like air exhaust scrubbers, or wastewater treatment systems, and did not require process- or equipment-specific treatment. In these cases, roadmapping that was paced by the two-year Tech development cycle was even more problematic. Factory systems tended to endure, and their optimization for an earlier process did not necessarily last. Changes in composition or concentrations of the exhaust could vastly alter the efficiency and effectiveness of such systems. Site environmental engineers were very concerned about how to size a new air exhaust system because its efficiency of pollutant removal depended strongly on the fab throughput and hence the volume of exhaust. Following a senior fab manager's presentation of throughput forecasts for each fab in which he admitted that the forecast was likely to change, the environmental engineers asked what they were to do about sizing their systems which were expected to operate for many years. Just 'march to the current version of the Long Range Plan,' the manager conceded.

Some EnviroTech and Tech managers felt that environmental work should get away from a process by process approach that was so tied to the development of individual manufacturing process steps, variations in chemical concentrations, exhaust volumes and output. One EnviroTech manager suggested that work should be directed towards the 'generic problems the industry has always had, instead of looking at process-specific problems.' It always comes down to the same type of issues, he argued, things like water use, certain chemicals and solvents. Indeed, some environmental roadmaps reflected this, with major categories for goals associated with water consumption, and factory site emissions of certain classes of chemicals. But like Tech roadmaps, efforts were also made to delineate specific equipment and operating parameters that would be needed to attain these goals.

Fitting these slightly different roadmaps together remained a challenge, as the earlier vignette of the 'roadmap review' portion of an EnviroCouncil meeting revealed. Gaining proficiency at roadmapping was a way for the EnviroCouncil not only to improve planning of environmental treatment, but also a way for them to demonstrate to others, especially those within Tech, that environmental issues could at least be somewhat subject to planning and control.

Summary: Environmental Work and Time

Like those in Tech, people engaged in environmental work experienced time as a critical, limited, resource. There was an urgency associated with most projects, and an effort was made to match many projects to the incessant pace of new process development. In many ways, however, environmental work did not and could not adhere to this sense of time – the time available to develop new process-specific environmental solutions was squeezed between the time when equipment and chemicals were fully settled on for the manufacturing process, and the time when a new manufacturing generation started to roll out to fabs. Where members of Tech had the experience of being in control of process development, even when unanticipated problems arose and development time was squeezed, EnviroTech experienced many more constraints. Their work was subject to decisions made in Tech, as well as external limits that could change rapidly, and were certainly never tied to an overarching pacing logic like Moore's Law.

Even the nature of the work – engaging in discussions with external stakeholders, or following the evolution of issues that arose outside Chipco – required members of EnviroTech to engage in what were seen organizationally as time-wasting activities – attending meetings to watch and listen, or gathering information that was not firm enough to drive decision-making. This perhaps led to the perception, expressed by one manager, that those outside Tech have less 'work output.' Against a backdrop of Tech culture where time was to be seized and exploited to produce specific, measurable results, anything else could easily be seen as a waste of time.

CULTURE AND ENVIRONMENTAL WORK

For those engaged in environmental work at Chipco, meanings associated with the physical world, roles and interactions, knowledge and time were strongly connected to each other, just as they were for members of Tech.

Table 5.2   Key cultural understandings surrounding environmental work

	Cultural understandings manifested in environmental work
Physical world	Somewhat technically controllable within parameters imposed by manufacturing Constraints mediated by outsiders
Roles and interactions	Roles less specialized; work aligns with issues as they emerge Efforts to routinize interactions Rules and criteria for success come from multiple sources, including external sources, or are ambiguous
Knowledge	Imperfect; unpredictable Subjective and contextual Does not readily support close control and replication
Time	Work pacing by technology development is artificial, but pervasive Limited, but not individually exploitable, resource

The key manifestations of the culture surrounding environmental work are summarized in Table 5.2. Work practices for EnviroTech and others were strongly shaped by organizational norms that showed up so clearly within Tech – work was goal-directed, data-driven, and accomplished through focus and disciplined planning, interaction was relatively limited and focused on the achievement of specific goals. But at the same time, environmental work was characterized by a greater degree of uncertainty and unpredictability that came with the nature of environmental impacts, their regulation, and the concerns of numerous outsiders. This gave those working on environmental issues a diminished sense of control relative to their counterparts in Tech and an enhanced sense of the political and provisional nature of much of their work. In the next chapter, I explore the moves they made to advance the environmental issues by using their increasing knowledge of the dominant cultural meanings.

NOTES

1. Recall that all personal names are pseudonyms.
2. Recall that MBP stands for 'Management By Plan,' or deliverable.
3. Recall that 'tool' is the common name for equipment used in the chip manufacturing process.
4. Recall that POR stands for 'Plan of Record,' and referred to any formally selected process equipment, procedure, or material.
5. It would be wrong to imply that Tech engineers must not also work within constraints imposed by other processing steps. In these cases, at least everyone is trying to optimize

around a small set of identical variables, such as process yield, reliability, and through-put. Disputes can be adjudicated using the same criteria.

6. WIP is work in progress, or the actual wafers that are put through the full series of process steps. It is distinct from wafers that are used to monitor the process or used to assess particular process steps and hence only run through a portion of the processing. In a manufacturing fab, WIP is what ends up as real product. In the development fab, WIP consists of 'full loop' test wafers that pass through all the process steps to evaluate the process under development.

7. The pollution prevention hierarchy is a commonly used tool that establishes most and least favorable alternatives to treating chemical waste. It typically is stated as (from most to least environmentally favorable): reduce, reuse, recycle, abate.

8. Smell is an inherently tricky thing to measure. Sometimes the human nose is an order of magnitude more sensitive to a smell than is a detector. Often a chemical will smell under some conditions but not others, or will smell bad to some people but not others. Threshold values for odor are recognized by Chipco engineers as an imperfect measure, but the only way to quantify odor.

9. Global warming potential is a measure of a greenhouse gas contribution to global climate change, relative to CO_2.

10. These gases became the subject of a voluntary agreement on PFCs negotiated by the World Semiconductor Council and mentioned in Chapter 1.

11. The US Environmental Protection Agency (EPA) maintains a list of 188 chemicals considered hazardous air pollutants (HAPs) and it establishes controls on the emission of these from industrial sources.

12. NOx emissions are a by-product of high temperature combustion of fossil fuels and are associated with the formation of acid rain. Increases in NOx emissions typically signal an increase in energy use for combustion.

6.   Getting environment 'in'

> The normative elements of social systems are contingent claims which have to
> be sustained and 'made to count' . . . in the contexts of actual encounters.
>
> (Giddens, 1984: 30)

Environmental work did not fit easily with Chipco's normal mode of work. It demanded reliance on forms of knowledge that could not be simply represented through 'data,' and responsiveness to unpredictable external demands. Neither of these were easily reconciled with Tech's work which was dominated by adherence to the pacing and predictability of Moore's Law. But members of EnviroTech and others did, over time, gain Tech's attention to and action on environmental issues. How did they get these issues in? How did they gain the ability to exercise influence? What strategies for action were used, and how did these develop or change over time?

With much less influence, relative to Tech, over the nature of 'problems' that were attended to in the course of manufacturing technology development, EnviroTech had to work through Tech's cultural categories to advance its issues. Recall from Chapter 3 that groups hold unequal abilities to manage meaning within a company; some subcultural categories hold more sway than others. In such circumstances, those with little say may seek to 'sell' issues to others to influence their attention and actions. The details of issue selling and its unfolding over time between groups that have unequal power are not well known (Dutton *et al.*, 2002), however. In this chapter I focus on a series of encounters between EnviroTech and Tech on particular projects,[1] to explore how the different meanings associated with the work of each group were negotiated in practice. I pay attention to how the cultural understandings described in the previous two chapters influenced how EnviroTech advanced the environmental issues over time and with what degree of success. Through some early failures and adjustments on subsequent encounters, members of EnviroTech learned about critical aspects of Tech's culture and became better able to craft their strategies for action to appeal to these.

This chapter, then, explores the processes of change through which those seeking to advance the environmental issues began to appropriate elements of the dominant group's culture for new ends. Using the lens of issue selling, the analysis demonstrates how members of EnviroTech gained skill at representing the environmental issues as different from Tech's typical concerns, but not *too* different. Through the use of particular moves, the group drew attention to important differences while also establishing Tech's dependence on the effective resolution of the environmental issues. In this way, EnviroTech gradually gained the ability to use the existing culture to its advantage, changing how Tech paid attention to environmental issues, without fundamentally changing Tech's culture.

I first describe my selection and analysis of the projects used to explore these changes over a six-year period. Following this, I focus on what EnviroTech did – the moves its members made – to advance the issues on particular projects, and the shift in the pattern of moves used over time. I revisit the key cultural meanings surrounding Tech's work and how these shaped its members' understanding of problems and appropriate solutions to frame the challenges facing EnviroTech's issue selling efforts. Three projects are then examined in more depth to analyze how EnviroTech learned through experience to tailor moves so that they successfully attracted Tech's attention and action. The final section of the chapter explains why certain moves effectively represented issues as 'problems' for Tech, and triggered work on solutions, while other moves did not.

TRACKING EFFORTS TO ADVANCE ENVIRONMENTAL ISSUES

I consider seven projects in detail in this chapter. Together, these projects spanned a six-year period and each was aimed at addressing some environmental aspect of a specific manufacturing process under development. It is important to note that a number of other projects were being pursued but were not included in this set. In order to assess interactions between Tech and EnviroTech, I focused on those projects that were tied to the development of a manufacturing process for the next manufacturing generation to be introduced to the fabs. This excluded a number of the activities in which EnviroTech was engaged, including projects focused on factory-scale changes that would influence a number of future manufacturing generations (for example, reductions in fab-wide water and energy consumption), and activities to develop strategic plans or models that would account for and track environmental performance metrics more broadly.

In identifying projects I used a working definition that was consistent with how Chipco parsed its work. Projects were initiated to attain a particular goal (for example, selection of a piece of equipment that met specified operating parameters). They had defined start and end points, often involved managers and engineers dedicated to that project, and their

Table 6.1   Project pseudonyms and brief description

Project	Project Description/Need
'Destructor'	Eliminate toxic chemical from liquid waste stream associated with newly developed high performance process step
'Greenhouse'	Control releases of specialized gases associated with global climate change over several future process generations
'Recycler'	Extend use of equipment to recycle a high volume process chemical for new process generation, or adopt an alternative approach to recycling or reusing the chemical
'Capturer'	Develop equipment to capture secondary air emissions associated with a technical approach piloted for the Greenhouse project
'Blue Skies'	Eliminate visible, yet non-toxic, air emissions plumes associated with certain process steps
'Decision Tool'	Develop a structured decision process to guide the EnviroCouncil's decision making on environmental process development projects
'Clean Air'	Significantly reduce hazardous air emissions associated with newly adopted process equipment

outputs contributed to the larger innovative effort of developing the new manufacturing process generation. Projects offer tangible settings for comparison of efforts to advance a related set of issues over time, and their differences enable contrasts to be drawn. As mentioned in Chapter 2, and consistent with other researchers (Hansen, 1999), I eliminated six very early stage projects from the analysis. Two further projects were eliminated because I lacked sufficient sources of data on them to triangulate my findings.[2] After eliminating these, I was left with the seven projects for analysis, which included both successes and failures. A brief description of each project and its pseudonym are given in Table 6.1.

Measuring Moves

Concerned with how each project proceeded and how members of EnviroTech sought to overcome challenges to the integration of environmental considerations into manufacturing process development, I coded the data on each project, as mentioned in Chapter 2, for moves used by those advancing the issue (what did they say and/or do?), as well as diagnoses (what was wrong?), and evaluations (how successful were any approaches taken?). The goal here was to understand what was done on particular projects, and how these moves varied across projects.

I used the working definition of 'moves' as distinctive units of situated interaction captured in speech or action (Goffman, 1981; Pentland, 1992) and 'diagnoses' as problem and issues attributions (Benford and Snow, 2000) made as those involved prepared and carried out their moves. A diagnosis coded as 'environmental', for example, included a communication between EnviroTech and site environmental specialists which expressed 'concern that there was not enough environmental and safety representation' on the project team and elaborated environmental concerns that needed attention on the Recycler project. Moves captured more direct interactions between EnviroTech and those they sought to influence. For example, a move coded as 'providing data' included an EnviroTech presentation that outlined decision criteria and offered specific recommendations ('a continuous [qqq]mL/min process with . . . on-site reprocessing') for the Recycler project.

Probing Projects

To understand EnviroTech's use of moves within particular projects, I coded the data by project and I simultaneously created a timeline of key events and decisions, and a context chart showing who was involved. The timing and duration of each project is shown in Figure 6.1 along with the timing of the formation of EnviroTech and the EnviroCouncil, and the earlier Strategic Environmental Policy Council (mentioned in Chapter 5). Note that the start date in Figure 6.1 indicates when a project was first initiated and the end date when an alternative environmental solution or alternative equipment adopted. Hence, for the earlier projects the timeline captures the development phase as well as the implementation of the equipment or solution in the fabs, if applicable.

It is important to note that, despite the formal creation of the EnviroTech group in the middle of the time period, individuals who would become members of this group were extensively involved in earlier projects. All but the earliest projects included at least one, and up to all, of the three managers who would run the EnviroTech group. This significant continuity allowed me to compare meaningfully the actions of those advancing the issues across projects.

As I analyzed each project, I modified and refined descriptions of the codes, ensuring that each type of move and diagnosis was consistent across its occurrences. Once I had settled on the codes, I analyzed the coded data across all of the projects over time in order to explore connections between moves made, the experiences of the interactions between EnviroTech and Tech, and outcomes of these interactions. This analysis connected back to the cultural meanings described in the two previous chapters and

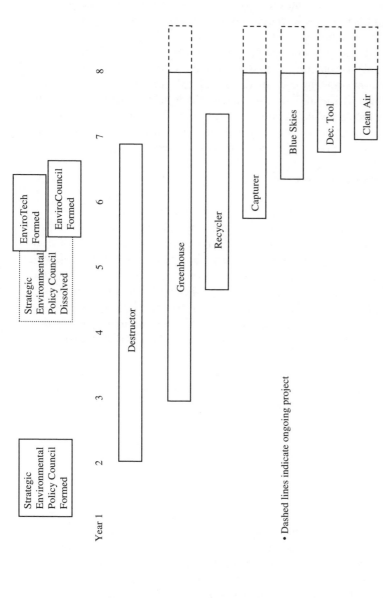

Figure 6.1   Project timing and formal structural changes[1]

[1] A modified version of this figure appears in J. Howard-Grenville (2007) 'Developing issue selling effectiveness over time: issue selling as resourcing,' *Organization Science* (forthcoming).

accounted for the observation that moves cannot be fully understood 'isolated from the situational particulars of the context . . . in which they occur' (Pentland, 1992: 530). This also led to the observation that the pattern of moves used shifted considerably over time and across projects, and helped me to locate explanations for this shift in what else was changing over the same time period.

Overall, the project analysis led to an understanding of how environmental problems were set, what strategies for action were used to work on them, and how and why each of these changed over time. It demonstrates that members of EnviroTech gained assets that helped them represent the environmental issues in ways that resonated with Tech's cultural categories, but, more importantly, that they learned through earlier experiences of failure and resistance to adjust their moves and representations.

Assessing Project Success

In order to assess the meaning of changes that occurred across the projects, it is of course essential to have some sense of the relative success of the various projects. I characterized the overall success or failure of each project using a composite of six measures: evaluations of satisfaction with the project outcome by (a) the proponents of the project (EnviroTech) and (b) the recipients of the project (Tech); (c) whether the environmental solution was ultimately adopted; (d) if adopted, whether it was implemented on-time (to integrate with the appropriate process technology); (e) whether the solution had met its environmental goals; and finally (f) whether it had met process goals. For example, the Destructor project was identified as a failure because, although it was adopted and implemented on time with the new process generation, its operation did not reliably meet environmental goals, it disrupted manufacturing and virtually everyone involved concluded it was a failure.

WHAT CHANGED?

A great deal changed over the time period covered by the seven projects. The EnviroTech group was formally created, even though its members had been playing similar roles less formally for some years. EnviroTech grew in size and somewhat in prominence. The nature of the problems that they set changed somewhat also. Perhaps most strikingly, the pattern of moves made by EnviroTech – what they actually did in their encounters with Tech – changed a lot. The shift in the pattern of moves used is captured in Table 6.2. Two moves, labeled 'providing data' and 'offering explanations,' were much

Table 6.2   Shift in moves used by project[1]

Moves	Destructor	Greenhouse	Recycler	Capturer	Blue Skies	Dec. Tool	Clean Air
Assert decision processes							
Take control	81%	74%	67%	67%	37%	50%	47%
Appeal to commitments							
Work within constraints							
Provide data	19%	26%	33%	33%	63%	50%	53%
Offer explanations							
Project Initiated	Year 2	Year 3	Year 4	Year 5	Year 6	Year 6	Year 7
Project Outcome	Failure	Failure	Failure	Failure	Success	Success	Success

[1] A modified version of this table appears in J. Howard-Grenville (2007) 'Developing issue selling effectiveness over time: Issue selling as resourcing', *Organization Science* (forthcoming).

more prevalent on later projects (comprising half or more of all moves used) than they were on earlier ones (comprising one-third or less of all moves used). The shift in moves accompanies a shift in project success. While all of the projects earlier in the time period failed to meet their intended goals, all of those initiated later in the time period achieved their intended goals, or at least got early support from within Tech.[3]

Before exploring why and how the shift in moves seemed to trigger a shift in project success, the moves themselves are described in more detail. 'Moves' are defined as discrete elements of interactions (Goffman, 1981; Pentland, 1992) and their use can express practical knowledge about how to advance issues effectively in an organization (Dutton *et al.*, 2001). In other words, moves are the units of action or interaction that may, or may not, comprise effective strategies for action within an organization's culture. It is important to consider the moves made by EnviroTech for these were the most immediate, day-to-day efforts made to integrate environmental issues in to the work of new manufacturing process development at Chipco.

Moves Made

Six different types of moves were used by EnviroTech in the seven projects studied. These moves included: asserting decision processes, taking control, appealing to commitments, working within constraints, providing data, and offering explanations. While each move was used on almost every project, there was a distinct shift in the pattern of moves used over time, as indicated in Table 6.2.

Asserting decision processes
This move involved expressing intended or actual adherence to Tech's formalized decision processes. For example, in giving an update on the Recycler project an EnviroTech manager was careful to note that the appropriate formal bodies had been consulted and procedures followed, stating that 'the decision was ratified by the [Tech] steering committee and now needs to be ratified by the JEM (Joint Engineering Management committee) and the [EnviroCouncil].'

Taking control
Central to this move was the initiation of rapid and decisive action on the issue. While this could be seen as contradictory to the more measured approach of deliberately and publicly adhering to Tech's decision processes, taking control was complementary in this context. Tech's decision processes existed to enable the rapid and accurate resolution of problems, and equally important to this end was an orientation to firmly take control

of and drive solutions. As a manager involved in the early stages of the Greenhouse project explained:

> When [Chipco] was first looking at [greenhouse gas emission] issues we didn't know whether we would have to do something or not, but we didn't want to be in a position of having to do something but not being ready with a technical solution.

Appealing to commitments

This move involved raising implications of the issue for compliance with Chipco's formal or informal environmental policies or regulatory obligations. For example, the team working on the Recycler project used input from environmental specialists to argue that abandoning the Recyclers would involve 'moving in the wrong direction on our most visible parameter, which might mitigate against achieving a [regulatory] license two or three years from now,' and that it would create an issue for 'site commitments to the county and community for aggressive pollution prevention.'

Working within constraints

With this move, pragmatic efforts were undertaken to understand and accommodate internal factors that influenced the type and timing of actions on an issue. For EnviroTech, this meant recognizing and accommodating constraints associated with the underlying process technology and its timing. For example, the decision in the Recycler project was influenced by an expected migration in process equipment to occur two generations out. An EnviroTech manager noted, 'we didn't foresee the use of [the Recycler] for [the generation after the next one] because of new wet benches,' so it 'ended up being a question of spending money to buy five to eight [Recyclers] for only the [next process generation].' Without an expectation of their continued use, it was that much harder to justify this investment in Recyclers and EnviroTech largely accepted this constraint posed by the process technology migration.

Providing data

This move involved collecting and sharing information to represent aspects of the new issue in detail. For EnviroTech, this took the form of sharing information on the current environmental performance, process performance, cost and other parameters, and making projections about these parameters under various alternatives. For example, the EnviroCouncil chair circulated an update on the Clean Air project as part of a weekly communication with other managers, noting:

> Significant progress has been made on recipe optimization ([chemical f] emissions of [xxx lbs/ws][4] are now at about [yyy lbs/ws]) and at identifying two

candidate technologies for emissions treatment which appear to operate at least at 95 percent removal efficiency.

While the data provided might implicitly account for environmental commitments or constraints, it tended to be conveyed as 'just the facts.' On the Recycler project, for example, one team member communicated:

> [An overseas fab] is currently close to the maximum salt ceiling with [Recycler] running. Removing [the Recycler] but going to [the new process generation] would increase [chemical S] effluent by approximately 2X.

Offering explanations

Related to providing data, this move involved presenting detailed interpretations and implications of issues to critical audiences. It differed from providing data in that it made explicit the reasons for one interpretation over another, or the need for one solution over another. In many cases, explanations were offered using terms and metrics familiar to the recipients, but potentially less well suited to the issue itself. For example, on the Clean Air project described in Chapter 1, while the EnviroCouncil communicated internally in terms of air emissions metrics (for example, 'the goal . . . is to reduce from [xxx lbs/ws] to [zzz lbs/ws]'), their communications to Tech and senior management were in terms that captured this audience's concerns about manufacturing capacity, asserting that 'current estimates of [hazardous air emissions] indicate a major constraint on site capacity, emissions are approximately $20X^5$ of the process goal.'

ISSUE SELLING AS A FRAMEWORK FOR CHANGE

Several of the moves used by EnviroTech resemble quite closely those identified in prior work on selling issues and exercising influence in organizations. As mentioned in Chapter 3, those seeking to influence the attention and actions of others within organizations often use rational persuasion, present issues using data and sound business logic, involve others, prepare carefully by educating themselves and assembling information about the issue and move opportunistically to try to advance issues when they might be most salient (Kipnis *et al.*, 1980; Yukl and Falbe, 1990; Dutton and Ashford, 1993; Dutton *et al.*, 2001).

The shift in moves used by EnviroTech suggests that successful issue selling does not come automatically, however. Why? Issue sellers typically hold little power relative to those they are trying to influence, and it takes time and repeated interaction to develop the ability to exercise influence in such settings. Issue sellers tend to operate from positions of disadvantage due to hierarchical or political constraints (Dutton *et al.*, 1997; Ashford *et al.*, 1998; Dutton *et al.*, 2001; Dutton *et al.*, 2002). Not only are they often lower in a company's formal hierarchy (as in EnviroTech's case), but they may be disadvantaged in terms of the company's informal power structure which is comprised of networks of communication, advice and expertise that can lead to differential status and opportunity.

The Relative Power of EnviroTech and Tech

It is clear from the previous two chapters that Tech and EnviroTech did not enjoy the same status within Chipco, putting EnviroTech at a significant disadvantage in its capacity to influence Tech's attention to environmental issues. The numbers alone are telling. Tech employed approximately 1500 engineers and managers; EnviroTech had grown in size to 11 engineers and managers by the time of my study. Counting the other environmental specialists employed in corporate and site EH&S as well as those in the Facilities group would bring the total close to 75,[6] but relatively few of these were primarily concerned with the environmental impact of manufacturing processes under development. Furthermore, EnviroTech had been formally established less than three years prior to my participant observation period, whereas Tech had been in existence for nearly 20 years. Though created to interface directly with Tech, EnviroTech did not directly report to Tech nor share its management structure, largely for historical reasons to do with prior formal roles of the three EnviroTech managers.[7] EnviroTech was also two levels lower in the formal hierarchy than Tech.

Power flows not just from a group's size and position in the hierarchy, but also from the centrality of the group's work to that of the company as a whole (Hickson *et al.*, 1971; Hinings *et al.*, 1974). By this measure also, Tech was dominant. Its actions and skills were central to the development and deployment of new manufacturing generations on the relentless two-year cycle, the key capability widely credited for Chipco's long-standing market success. Through its norm of identical replication of manufacturing processes across the fabs, Tech's decisions and actions were strongly embedded in the manufacturing technology itself, making it virtually impossible for others 'downstream' to represent their interests or introduce changes, a further source of power (Carlile, 2004). Finally, the perceived expertise and status of Tech's members contributed symbolically to the group's power (Van Maanen and Barley, 1985).

In contrast, EnviroTech enjoyed only relatively fleeting centrality – a handful of incidents had elevated environmental issues to the level that justified the creation of EnviroTech and the EnviroCouncil, but most members of Tech and other groups remained largely unaware of their existence. At the time of the study, their work remained quite firmly down-stream of Tech's in practice. The EnviroCouncil continued to receive news of process details much later than it ought to, often after critical equipment and chemical choices had been made. Even the expertise of EnviroTech members to be involved in process decisions was questioned; recall the Tech manager remarking that he had little faith in data presented by EnviroTech because no one in the group 'had ever been inside a fab.'

Perhaps more important even than these formal and informal differences in the positions of the groups and perceptions of their work was the role each group played in the construction of meaning within the company. To what extent does one group set the 'ground rules' that other groups must follow? As explained in Chapter 3, different groups in an organization can have different subcultures – patterns of meaning reproduced through their actions – and some of these may play a very prominent role in the organization as a whole, while others may not. This may lead to the actions and norms of one group continually legitimating certain types of issues, without the obvious exercise of formal authority (Hardy, 1994; Phillips, 1997). The result has been called 'invisible' agenda-setting or 'non-decision making,' a pervasive form of power (Bacharach and Baratz, 1963; Lukes, 1974; Ranson *et al.*, 1980) that is particularly relevant to understanding the challenges issue sellers face in general and in, specifically, the challenges that EnviroTech faced in advancing the environmental issues at Chipco.

While it implicitly recognizes that issue sellers operate from positions of disadvantage (Ashford *et al.*, 1998; Dutton *et al.*, 2001; Dutton *et al.*, 2002), the work on issue selling does not specifically address how hierarchical, political or cultural constraints are experienced by issue sellers, and how the moves they make do (or do not) overcome these. Looking at the series of interactions between Tech and EnviroTech across the seven projects enables an understanding of how EnviroTech was able to construct influential moves (or not), why certain moves were more effective than others given the hierarchical and subcultural differences, and how EnviroTech adopted new patterns of moves over time. To do this, it is first necessary to briefly revisit the core meanings in Tech's culture for these informed what constituted a 'problem' for Tech and what types of solutions it tended to favor. These were the core norms against which EnviroTech's issues and actions were judged.

'Problems' and 'Solutions' According to Tech

The nature of Tech's work, and the cultural meanings associated with it, described in Chapter 4, resulted in distinctive understandings by its members of what comprised a problem and what comprised a solution.

Problems were things that impeded the development or operation of effective, reliable manufacturing processes. Recall the comment made by one Tech manager: '[Chipco] tends to focus on things that limit [manufacturing] performance.' Practical, technical, and data-driven problems were those considered the norm. Members of Tech and Manufacturing manipulated the material world on a precise scale, exercised exquisite control over it, and replicated this control in fabs dispersed around the globe. Their specialized roles and interactions, preferences for data as the sources of practical knowledge, and focused and disciplined work practices to achieve measurable goals fit with these experiences of the physical world, and recreated an experience of the work as technically challenging, but by and large predictable and controllable. With these cultural understandings, the problems members of Tech set for themselves were focused on technical limitations. Such problems were solvable through focus, hard work and the deployment of technical expertise.

As the Clean Air project described in Chapter 1 demonstrated, the key reason that EnviroTech became successful at gaining Tech's attention and action on the issue was because it had presented the problem as a Tech problem, one that posed a key manufacturing constraint. Furthermore, they approached the solution as a Tech solution, focused on a technical approach that solved the immediate problem in the time available. The moves used most heavily on this project, providing data and offering explanations, enabled them to portray the problem in a way that triggered Tech's attention. In the next section, I explore two projects that preceded Clean Air in some detail in order to trace what else was changing that led EnviroTech to learn about and ultimately adopt a more effective pattern of moves for selling the environmental issues.

PATTERNS OF CHANGE: EXAMINING THREE PROJECTS

Two shifts occurred over the six years studied that enabled EnviroTech to become more successful at influencing Tech by representing the new issues as problems for this core group. The first shift was simply the formal creation of EnviroTech, and some growth in its number of members and their expertise. This gave the individuals involved several assets that could serve as sources of power during their interactions with Tech. Consistent with seeing power as having multiple dimensions (formal, informal and inherent in dominant cultural meanings), there are several potential assets that issue sellers can draw on as they try to construct influential moves: formal authority (the ability to mobilize people or money), relationships (existence and quality of relationships, particularly those outside formal authority structures), expertise (related to the content of the issues, such as technical knowledge), and normative knowledge (related to 'how to get things done' or practical knowledge of the prevailing organizational norms) (Dutton *et al.*, 2001; Feldman, 2004). Starting from a position of severely limited assets of formal authority, relationships, expertise and normative knowledge on the earliest project studied, the Destructor project, those advancing the environmental issues gained assets of each type over time. It is important to remember that these assets are only potentials, however, unless they are successfully drawn upon in particular interactions.

This relates to the second shift observed over time: members of EnviroTech learned from difficult interactions and early failures which moves were ineffective at influencing Tech and why. Generally, patterns of moves that were ineffective were those that failed to trigger Tech's 'problem' interpretations, while those that were effective did so. Moves that portrayed the environmental issues as 'too different' failed to trigger attention and action; somewhat ironically, moves that failed to portray the environmental issues as 'different enough' also failed. The most effective pattern of moves seemed to strike a balance in how the issues were represented – similar enough that Tech understood them as 'constraints,' yet different enough that unique aspects of the problem were appropriately addressed. This is illustrated more fully through a description of the interactions on the Destructor project (initiated earliest in the time period), the Recycler project (initiated in the middle of the time period), and a recap of the Clean Air project (initiated late in the time period).

The Destructor Project

The Destructor project involved the development of equipment to remove (and destroy) a toxic chemical present in waste 'slurry' (a solid/liquid mixture) produced by a highly successful and newly developed manufacturing process step. Regulation governed the release of the chemical, although even environmental specialists questioned internally 'whether [treatment] made sense because [the] bound [chemical compound] was so stable,' that it was virtually undetectable. But, to one Tech manager, the more important matter was 'the name, it sounds scary.' He added, 'people would be concerned about any waste containing [the chemical].' The environmental considerations, therefore, were never highly elaborated; all involved agreed that some sort of treatment system was needed.

Time was tight with Tech working hard to 'get the slurry and tool (equipment) right' so the new process could be deployed with the new manufacturing generation. A Tech engineer noted that 'There was a cursory review of the alternative technologies but they didn't have much time . . . they needed an environmental solution in a couple of months.' A Facilities engineer was put in charge of selecting equipment (a 'Destructor') that would destroy the target chemical, and installing it in the development fab for pilot testing. As one Tech manager put it, 'We had a tool, had it in the basement and [the Facilities engineer] managing it, so we thought we were done.'

But they were far from done. The Destructor equipment was plagued by operational problems, as pipes plugged and burst, causing safety as well as environmental hazards. To meet the relentless schedule for implementing the new manufacturing generation, 16 Destructor units were ultimately installed in four fabs over four years. Fabs were shut down periodically while problems with Destructor operations were addressed. In some cases the chemical waste had to be shipped off site to a waste handler while Destructors underwent more significant repair.

Many blamed the failures of the Destructor units on insufficient attention to the standard procedures and norms of process development during the pilot testing stage. 'There was no burn in on the [Destructor] unit, it was not operated at maximum capacity [to test reliability for a real manufacturing setting],' reflected one engineer. The project was not adequately resourced, as one Tech manager noted, '[the Facilities group] didn't have the resources, they use one engineer to support a whole lot of systems (gave five examples).' Allegations were even made that those involved did not meet Tech's standards for focus, dedication, and thoroughness: 'Pressure disks were put in backwards despite being labeled front and back! That's just the tip of the iceberg in terms of problems'; '[Tech] gave [Facilities] money to buy spare parts and six months later they were still trying to write the PO [Purchase Order]; if this had been [Tech] it would have been done in an afternoon.' One Tech engineer summarized his impressions of the Destructor experience by suggesting that 'to make the system bulletproof, everything has to be run like [Tech].'

How had the problem gone from one that everyone involved – Tech included – agreed needed to be solved, to one whose solution continued to be held up even years later as an example of what should not be repeated?

Assets on the Destructor project
First, those who initially developed the Destructor equipment and worked with Tech to deploy it to the manufacturing fabs with the new process step had extremely limited assets of formal authority, relationships, expertise, and normative knowledge to draw on. This project preceded the formal creation of EnviroTech. A number of engineers who worked on the project would eventually join EnviroTech upon its creation, but at the time of the project they had no formal role in systematically addressing environmental

issues associated with process development. Further, several of the key people involved were from the Facilities group whose members maintained and operated equipment to support fab operations. They were not typically asked to get involved in developing new equipment, and their expertise and resources were not tailored to do so. This is reflected in some of the comments made (mentioned above) about the competence (or lack thereof) of the work (for example, the pressure disks put in backwards) and the number of systems engineers in the group were expected to support. A lack of respect for the expertise of the Facilities group and the poor state of relations between Tech and Facilities are summed up in this Tech manager's comment: 'I realize now that [Facilities] was not organized or capable to do this. Their techs [technicians] don't hold a candle to our techs.' Finally, those who worked on the project (from Facilities as well as a handful of other groups) had limited experience working with Tech. Their lack of normative knowledge about how to 'get things done' is reflected in the Tech manager's criticism about their ability to order spare parts (mentioned above).

Moves made on the Destructor project

From this position, it seems quite understandable that the group working on the Destructor project appeared to largely work from a 'defensive' stance once the problems cropped up. That is, they worked very hard to convince others that they had adopted Tech's standard approaches for diagnosing technical problems and fixing them. With the poorly functioning Destructors posing an immediate threat to the normal operation of the manufacturing fabs, Tech and Manufacturing became quite heavily involved and also imposed their standard approaches. Several years after the Destructor equipment was first developed, a Joint Engineering Team (JET) was formed that drew engineers from the Tech, Facilities and (the now newly created) EnviroTech groups to address the problems. The key move – asserting decision processes – used on this project (see Table 6.2) represents efforts by the JET and others to closely mimic Tech's standard approaches, perhaps to redress impressions of incompetence and poor execution associated with the initial lack of assets.

The 'problem' on the Destructor project

While the limited assets of those who initially developed the Destructor certainly contributed to its failures, we can learn more about what went wrong on this project by considering the nature of the problem that was set up from the outset. As mentioned, the environmental considerations were never highly elaborated on this project. Those involved overwhelmingly described the nature of the problems as, first, a result of unreliable technology, and second, poor management once operational problems were encountered. Even late in the project a Tech manager noted that 'It was never an environmental problem, in fact, I don't think they ever had a detectable level of [the chemical] in five years . . . but it was a design problem, an engineering problem.' The Destructor problems became urgent when they began to impede the normal operation of the factory. One Tech manager reflected that they 'never had a problem with the [Destructor] doing what it was supposed to do, but it didn't meet availability or reliability goals [for the fab].'

Consistent with their understanding of problems as things that limited manufacturing performance, and their emphasis on focused, disciplined work, Tech managers and engineers also asserted that the Destructor problems could have been overcome with the aggressive application of resources and hard work. One Tech manager admitted that,

> We dropped the ball on the [Destructors]. If they had staffed it from the beginning the way they staffed [process] stuff, I am convinced we would not have had a problem.

Another noted that 'We can make [the technology] work; availability etc. are manageable if properly resourced.'

The recycling system I observed with Irene (see Chapter 5) was developed to address some of the problems with the Destructors. As a result, it was valued within Tech and Manufacturing not for its environmental benefits as much for its potential to reduce the burden on the Destructors and hence improve their reliability. Recycling would also reduce the total slurry cost, which was very high, and could reduce the capital cost of new Destructors for fabs not yet using them. One Tech manager said 'Recycling would save $5 million a year for Chipco, and should also help the [Destructor] systems with less plugging of the reactor because about half the amount of stuff would be going into it.' Adding that recycling had been briefly considered some years earlier when the process technology was first introduced, he noted that, at that time, 'it was never a priority.' 'Waste treatment wasn't considered a showstopper,' he added, observing that 'there was a lot of other work to get the slurry and tool right. We were running 10 000 wafers . . . with tweezers [that is, by hand and on an individual basis].' Even once the process was fully deployed and recycling the slurry was an attractive way to reduce the impact of the Destructor problems, it was hard to convince other fabs to consider recycling. 'One of the problems with fixing the [Destructors] is that [the new process for which the system is needed] has been so tremendously successful . . . that no one wants to touch it,' observed one manager, reflecting a more general conservatism associated with changing well-functioning manufacturing processes.

Why the Destructor Project Failed

The most proximate cause of failure on the Destructor project – that the equipment was developed by a group that lacked the resources and skill to do so and hence was poorly designed and technically inadequate to stand up to continuous manufacturing use – tells only part of the story. A deeper reason for the failure of this project can be seen by considering how the problems set around the project – both during the Destructor's development and once its technical inadequacies were revealed – blinded those involved to certain key issues. Characterizing the problem as one of technical design masked the novelty associated with the environmental treatment of a new chemical. The consequences of this were only made clear once the Destructors had been deployed to the fabs, and too far into the project to make significant changes. One EnviroTech engineer who had been involved in the JET observed that, 'at first there was very little fundamental understanding of the underlying mechanisms of the [chemical] treatment.' Another JET engineer noted that 'the . . . technology was new to the company' and people 'thought this was a high temperature high pressure system but it wasn't . . . it shows [Chipco's] inexperience with such equipment.'

Downplaying the differences introduced by the new chemical itself, by failing to elaborate on the environmental issue at the outset and consider the particular challenges posed in treating it, made the problem appear as a familiar one of equipment development. And the key moves which brought standard Tech approaches to bear on the problem only reinforced the sense that this was simply a poorly executed equipment development project. A Tech manager reflected that 'It became very clear that [equipment like the Destructor] is absolutely fundamental to the success of the fab.' But this evaluation only reinforced Tech's approach to problem solving. One Tech manager concluded, 'If we had to do it again, [Tech] would have owned the waste system.'

Ironically, the experiences on the Destructor project did trigger a key 'problem' for Tech when the malfunctioning equipment became a constraint on manufacturing, and hence it was a way for the environmental issues to come to the attention of the group and move them to action. But the action involved reasserting Tech's dominant strategies for action, ignoring and even masking other approaches that might have led to environmentally more favorable outcomes, such as recycling or other treatment methods that addressed the challenges of dealing with this particular chemical. While the Destructor project can be characterized as *under*-representing what was distinctive and new about addressing an environmental impact of a manufacturing process, and hence missing an opportunity to pursue a workable solution, the subsequent Recycler project can be characterized as *over*-representing differences associated with environmental impacts, and hence closing off a potential opportunity to develop a solution.

The Recycler Project

The Recycler project centered on a decision to adopt equipment to recycle a high-volume chemical for reuse in a manufacturing process step, or to reduce consumption of the chemical through some other means. A few years earlier, some Recycler equipment had been adopted for a previous manu-facturing generation, a decision that was, according to one EnviroTech manager, a 'no-brainer, it increased productivity (by reducing downtime), and decreased [chemical] down the drain.' It also saved money, reducing spending on a very high volume material that cost $28 per gallon.[8] Several years later, however, changes in the underlying manufacturing process, and a resulting severe reduction in the volume of chemical used, had led to calls to discontinue the use of Recyclers for future process generations.

In contrast to the early work on the Destructor, the decision process undertaken on the Recycler project was extensive, deliberate and inclusive. Five alternatives were considered by a team that drew on expertise from ten functional areas and seven of Chipco's geographical sites. The team established explicit decision criteria and ranked their relative importance, and environmental performance was among them. The team's chair, an EnviroTech manager, was clear in his commitment to mimic Tech's decision processes and told the team, 'I will be working to drive to one method for all [Chipco] sites.' While the decision process was often contentious with deep divisions over the tradeoffs between the environmental and other goals, the chair took great pains to communicate to others that a sound decision process based on data was being followed, as was standard within Tech. At one point to dispel rumors that a decision had been made without adequate analysis, he wrote a clarification of the status of the project and added at the end, 'NO DECISION HAS YET BEEN MADE' (emphasis in original).

At the same time, environmental considerations were explicitly injected into the analysis. One environmental specialist questioned, 'Isn't this pro-posal contrary to the long term strategic objective of minimizing environ-mental impact regardless of whether we are inside our license or not?' He added, 'it is moving in the wrong direction on our most visible parameter, which might mitigate against achieving a [regulatory] license two or three years from now.' Another indicated that her fab 'could probably accom-modate [a switch away from the Recycler]' but it would create an issue for 'site commitments to the county and community for aggressive pollution prevention.'

In the end, however, others on the team remained unconvinced of the need to address the environmental impacts, noting that 'the ultimate question is do we need [chemical recycling]' and asserting the validity of other decision criteria and procedures: 'the finance people are doing a model that will show there is no ROI.' One Manufacturing manager sought 'an absolute ruling, legal or otherwise' on Chipco's 'real risks (not perceived)' of having a chemical supplier 'come in and take out [the chemical] in a tanker truck and sell it off to someone outside of [Chipco]' as opposed to using the Recycler. This prompted an environmental manager to reply angrily that 'the liability potential is not "perceived." It is real . . .!!'

In an effort to address these concerns, the team's chair suggested relying on further analysis. He summarized, 'Since the original reason for [the Recycler] was environmentally driven we will attempt to analyze the environmental cost of ownership using the new [third party] model to see if the environmental costs could influence the ROI.' Reasserting the team's adherence to standard Tech decision-making approaches that relied on data and analysis, this statement nonetheless captures the fact that environmental criteria were – perhaps for the first time – explicitly being considered as part of that analysis.

Assets on the Recycler project

The Recycler project was initiated as EnviroTech and the EnviroCouncil were formally being created. A new-found authority to introduce environmental criteria into process related decisions flowed from this and served as a key potential asset on this project. However, at this stage, only three managers and three engineers made up the EnviroTech group and their expertise was centered on environmental and facility-related aspects of manufacturing, not drawn from participation in the manufacturing process or in technology development projects. They also had few relationships with those in Tech, and the EnviroTech group itself was highly dispersed geographically with none of its members located at Tech's primary site. The effort made by the Recycler project team's chair (an EnviroTech manager) to follow Tech's norms for decision making demonstrates an increase in the normative knowledge held by those seeking to advance environmental issues, as compared to the earlier Destructor project.

Moves made on the Recycler project

The predominant moves on the Recycler project, appealing to commitments and asserting decision processes (see Table 6.2), suggest that the group sought to strike a balance between explicitly introducing environmental commitments and criteria for consideration and also adhering to

Tech's standard norms for decision making. The most heavily used move, appealing to commitments, brought the environmental considerations front and center. While environmental specialists at times expressed the environmental goal (recycling the chemical) in a way that indicated potential future impacts on manufacturing ('might mitigate against achieving a [regulatory] license two or three years from now'), such statements were not forcefully or consistently made, nor did they contain 'data' of the type that might convince members of Tech and Manufacturing of their importance. By and large, the environmental considerations were stated on their own terms, referencing Chipco's earlier commitment to recycling this chemical, and the need to continue to demonstrate this commitment to the communities in which it operated.

The 'appealing to commitments' move in particular represented a significant departure in what was done to advance the environmental considerations, relative to the earlier Destructor project where very little was ever said about the environmental nature of the problem and its importance. Indeed, on the Destructor project the lack of attention to the novelty that the new chemical and its environmental treatment introduced led to a collective inability to develop an appropriate solution. But on the Recycler project the sustained and explicit attention to the novel (for a technology development project) environmental criteria seemed to backfire, for it resulted in an unwillingness to address the environmental issues absent in other criteria.

The 'problem' on the Recycler project
Through their moves of both appealing to commitments and asserting decision criteria, the group advancing the issue sought to represent it as one among many criteria that would lead to an environmental approach (recycling or some other form of chemical reuse) that was also economic and appropriate for the manufacturing process. The recipients of the issue – including members of the decision team from Tech and Manufacturing – failed to see the problem in the same light. For these people, the Recyclers were not regarded as a solution to a problem for there was no 'problem' to begin with. One Manufacturing managers' comments reflect a fundamental lack of acceptance of a connection between addressing the environmental issues and attaining any other valued goals:

> WHY SHOULD WE [RECYCLE]? We should [recycle] when it is the right thing to do for [Chipco]. We should [recycle] when it is the right thing to do for the process. We should [recycle] when it is the right thing to do for the environment. We should [recycle] when the payback shows a good return on our investment. SHOULD WE [RECYCLE] WHEN NONE OF THE ABOVE ARE MET? (emphasis in original).

The problem to be addressed on the Recycler project was consistently characterized in opposing terms by different people involved. More than two-thirds of the problem attributions (coded as diagnoses) on this project were about environmental concerns (35 percent of the total) or cost concerns (39 percent of the total) and they almost exclusively were represented as trade-offs (even by those advancing various environmental solutions).

Not surprisingly, the moves did not generate the desired action for EnviroTech. After many meetings, a decision was reached to reuse the waste chemical in another (less environmentally efficient) way within the fab infrastructure, rather than install new Recyclers. Several years later, the required infrastructure changes were incomplete at several sites, and the reuse approach was eventually formally dropped in response to a company-wide call for cost-cutting.

Why the Recycler Project Failed

The Recycler project, and the subsequent decision to reuse the chemical on site (but not in a manufacturing process), ultimately failed not because people didn't know about the environmental impacts, but because these impacts never became consequential for those outside EnviroTech and the EH&S group. The comment made by the Manufacturing manager ('Why should we [recycle]?') reflects this and captures the lack of connection between the environmental goals and other concerns of those in Tech and Manufacturing. In one sense, the novelty introduced by explicitly attending to environmental considerations in the Recycler decision process may have backfired, by serving to represent the issues as 'too different' from the core concerns of others in the company. The final project discussed, Clean Air, appears to capture the environmental issues as 'different enough' that they get addressed appropriately, but not too different that others fail to accept their legitimacy.

The Clean Air Project

Recall that the Clean Air project, described in some detail in the opening chapter, arose when it became clear, very late in a process development cycle, that air emissions from newly selected process equipment exceeded an internally established goal by a factor of 20. While members of EnviroTech characterized it as potentially 'the biggest environmental problem we have ever faced,' they took pains to portray the problem in terms that appealed to those within Tech and Manufacturing. Complexities associated with treating the emissions stream were significant, but the main message EnviroTech sent was that, untreated, the problem posed a major threat to future manufacturing output. This got the attention of those at all levels within Tech, and EnviroTech was able to secure significant support (in both engineers and money) to work jointly on developing a technical solution. The Clean Air project stood out as the first environmental process development project for which a solution was demonstrated ahead of schedule.

Assets on the Clean Air project

EnviroTech's assets had changed considerably from the earlier projects, no doubt enabling them to engage more effectively with Tech on this project. First, both EnviroTech and the EnviroCouncil had been formally established for two years at the time that the Clean Air issue arose, so their formal authority was better established and at least some members of Tech were aware of their existence and their goals. They had grown in size to 11 members (three managers, eight engineers or technicians) and several of the newly acquired engineers had experience either in a manufacturing fab or working in Tech. This served to bolster their expertise as a group and the nature of their relationships with Tech. While their relational assets were still limited, some of the EnviroTech or EnviroCouncil members had brought with them or developed close ties with some members of Tech. Finally, EnviroTech's normative knowledge had increased through its experiences on earlier projects. The portrayal of the environmental issue in the Clean Air project suggests a more sophisticated and strategic approach to engage Tech's interests than the earlier efforts of either appealing explicitly to environmental commitments and/or asserting decision processes.

Despite these significant improvements in EnviroTech's assets, the group still lacked the standing to be treated as equal to Tech in decision making. The fact that they were made aware of the Clean Air problem so late in Tech's development cycle shows that EnviroTech still operated from a position of significant disadvantage. One manager told the EnviroCouncil 'we have only had a week to understand this problem . . . we got blindsided.' Discussions on the equipment itself had been going on for months at various TechCouncils. This and other projects led an EnviroTech manager to reflect that, 'most of what we do are still tack-on solutions.'

Moves made on the Clean Air project

Despite this, members of EnviroTech had accumulated the expertise and normative knowledge that enabled them to make a pattern of moves dominated by providing data and offering explanations (see Table 6.2). Providing data detailed the types of constraints posed by addressing the environmental goal. For example, an EnviroTech engineer reporting on the problem noted that they would need to develop equipment that was 96 percent efficient at removing the air emissions, was able to treat another hazardous material present, and that no known technologies were available to do so. Not only did this portray environmental issues as 'data-driven' rather than primarily corporate commitments or community concerns, but it also demonstrated EnviroTech's ability to collect and make sense of detailed technical data, an activity that was so central to Tech's work. In talking about the problem, some EnviroTech members expressed detailed knowledge of existing and proposed process chemistries and the constraints and tradeoffs these posed, and often reported on actual and target numerical metrics associated with the emissions reduction effort. The second heavily used move on this project, offering explanations, was related to providing data but also put the data into perspective and offered an interpretation of it that was relevant to the recipient. Recall from Chapter 1 that, in communicating with Tech, EnviroTech presented a chart depicting potential limitations on manufacturing capacity (in terms of 'wafer starts,' a key throughput metric, not in terms of air emissions themselves), if the emissions went untreated. This supported their framing of the problem as the 'first time the environmental implications are the biggest technical hurdle to bringing [new manufacturing equipment] in.'

The 'problem' on the Clean Air project

Like the Recycler project, diagnoses of the nature of the problem varied for this project. Almost three-quarters of the coded diagnoses either centered on environmental concerns (32 percent of the total) or on associated technology or process concerns (42 pecent of the total). However, unlike the Recycler project where these different attributions were in direct conflict with each other, the environmental and technology issues in the Clean Air project were presented as tied to each other. Addressing one involved addressing the other.

Representing the environmental issues in this way made them not only a familiar type of 'problem' for Tech, but also made them solvable. The mode of work adopted to address the Clean Air emissions issue was very similar to Tech's normal approach to technical challenges during process development – put a technical task force on it, give them the goals and resources, and get out of the way so they can pursue their goals with single-minded focus.

Why the Clean Air Project Succeeded

Addressing the excessive air emissions in the Clean Air project *was* critical to ensuring that the new process equipment could be deployed to the manufacturing fabs without delay. The sense of urgency and the nature of the problem were not simply constructed by EnviroTech. But the way in which the problem itself and its urgency were conveyed may well have had a lot to do with how it was received by those within Tech, accepted as relevant and legitimate, and ultimately worked on. EnviroTech's increased assets and their increased use of specific moves (providing data and offering explanations) enabled them to set the environmental problem as a Tech problem, and gain action on it. Rather than failing to represent the novelty and differences relevant to addressing the environmental issue (as in the Destructor case), or over-representing them so they appeared irrelevant to the concerns of others (as in the Recycler case), the actions taken on the Clean Air project struck a balance that captured the novelty associated with the environmental considerations while making them meaningful to others. This representation, enabled by the assets EnviroTech had acquired (most importantly, expertise and normative knowledge) and the particular moves they chose to make, was key to tapping into key cultural meanings prevalent in Tech that resulted in Tech seeing the issue as its own type of problem.

WHY THE CHANGE?

Taken together, the project data suggests that environmental considerations were successfully integrated when those advancing the new issues were able to represent what was novel and different about the issue, but, critically, connect this to dominant cultural understandings of what constituted a problem and, in particular, a solvable problem. Eventually, EnviroTech was able to sell issues to Tech, but issue selling in this case wasn't simply about drawing attention to new issues. It also involved overcoming some significant differences in the specialized knowledge and interests of each group. The latter is particularly difficult, as research on product development, innovation and other work across 'organizational boundaries' suggests (Dougherty, 1992; Bechky, 2003; Carlile, 2004).

Difference and Dependence

To effectively integrate knowledge and interests across boundaries between functional or other organizational groups, two characteristics in particular must be addressed: difference and dependence (Carlile and Rebentisch, 2003; Carlile, 2004). Difference includes differences in the type or quantity of specialized knowledge or expertise members bring to an interaction (Carlile, 2004) and it may show up in the language or metrics used, technical or other requirements associated with the work, and associated criteria used for evaluation. Dependencies include the extent of one group's dependence on another's (or a number of others') expertise, knowledge, or work

outputs in order to accomplish its work (Carlile, 2004). Difference captures
the 'gap' between the cultural understandings held by the issue sellers and
recipients, and dependence captures whether and to what extent this gap
matters to accomplishing the goals of each group. These concepts are
important here because the actions on each of the three projects described
in detail represented difference and dependence in quite different ways, and
with important consequences.

On the Destructor project, neither differences nor dependencies were
exposed by the moves made by those attempting to address the environmental issues. Both difference and dependence were present, however, and
dependence (of Tech and Manufacturing on a working environmental
treatment system) became eminently clear when the Destructors failed.
Heavy and largely unsuccessful reliance on standard Tech approaches as
the 'fix' on this project suggest a kind of failure that is common when new
differences and dependencies go unrecognized and existing practices are
reused without being adjusted to account for the new knowledge or requirements (Carlile, 2004). Moves used on the Recycler project, in contrast,
revealed significant differences between EnviroTech's representation of the
problem and that of Tech and Manufacturing. Indeed, the difference or gap
between the understandings held by these groups was too large and the
groups remained highly polarized in their interpretations and evaluations
of the issue. Dependence was not established through EnviroTech's moves
on the Recycler project so the issue remained inconsequential for Tech.
Only on the Clean Air project were both difference and dependency
revealed during interaction. By providing detailed data on the air emissions
and challenges associated with their treatment EnviroTech demonstrated
how the requirements for this issue differed from what was typical within
Tech, but by offering explanations they put these requirements in terms that
represented them as highly relevant problems for Tech.

Effective issue selling at Chipco seemed to demand that both differences
and dependencies were revealed through interactions on a project.
Difference without dependence risked painting an issue as too far 'out
there' as the Recycler project suggested. On the other hand, dependence
without difference might result in an issue being 'captured' by a recipient
group as if it was their own, with the result that the solution invoked may
fail to address novel requirements associated with the issue. The postscript
to the Clean Air project illustrates this latter risk. With the adopted
solution, the chemical removed from the air emissions would go through
multiple transformations (from gas to liquid, liquid to solid and solid to
landfill) before its eventual disposal. Recall from Chapter 1 that EnviroTech
ultimately wanted to recover the gas and recycle it directly, a much
more environmentally efficient approach. But this was, according to one

EnviroTech manager, 'a three- to five-year [project]' that would proceed separately as it failed to fit into Tech's dominant mode of work. With the immediate technical solution secured for the Clean Air project, members of Tech seemed oblivious to the longer-term problem of optimizing the environmental treatment. One Tech engineer gave an update on the Clean Air project with the pollution prevention hierarchy, 'Reduce, Reuse, Recycle, Abate,' running across the top of each presentation slide, but he seemed unmoved by the fact that the bulk of his presentation focused on the technical details of abatement tools proposed for adoption, the least environmentally desirable solution in the hierarchy. Here the full novelty of addressing the environmental issues was subsumed under the immediate need to remove a constraint on manufacturing and do so in the most technically efficient way.

Acquiring Assets and Learning from Failure

Difference and dependence can be used to illuminate the various outcomes EnviroTech obtained in seeking to sell its issues to Tech, but they cannot alone say much about how EnviroTech came to be able to represent difference and dependence adequately. For this, we need to consider what was changing or accumulating as EnviroTech and its precursors sought to advance the environmental issues. Indeed, skillfully representing difference and dependence in a way that triggered problems for Tech and hence their attention and action did not come automatically for EnviroTech. Both of the shifts documented through the descriptions of the three projects – changes in EnviroTech's assets and changes in their representations of the problems due to earlier difficult interactions or failures – contribute to explanations of how the group became more effective at issue selling. The assets acquired enabled EnviroTech to launch new moves. For example, as the group grew in numbers and gained some engineers with Tech experience, it undoubtedly became better able to collect and provide data. The adjustments EnviroTech made in how it represented issues and the moves it selected from a growing repertoire suggest that it was learning from its earlier experiences how to best influence Tech.

Within a single project there is also evidence that EnviroTech learned from resistance and actively adjusted its moves in response to earlier challenges. Consider the following examples from the Blue Skies project which was undertaken successfully and around the same time as the Clean Air project. In discussions among their project team, environmental specialists labeled community concern over visible, but harmless emission plumes as 'emotive' for certain communities, exchanged anecdotes about public queries regarding the plumes, and observed that 'the public affairs people don't want to have to explain it anymore.' But following a presentation where others questioned spending money on the equipment simply to address a public perception issue (one Manufacturing manager challenged that '[Chipco] would get better press by putting the money into local schools'), the team provided the following justification:

> [Chemical N] reacts with [chemicals F and C] to form visible plumes, typically when [chemical F or C] > 1 ppm (current average is 0.5 ppm), so plumes are an intermittent problem. Scrubber performance is poor in the presence of [chemical N] and this is complicated by the dilution of the exhaust . . . [the first reason for the Blue Skies project is] to improve house scrubber performance (currently averages [xx]% and should be above [yy]%).

The issue of public concern was addressed later in the presentation, following more data on emissions. The intentional manipulation of the message suggests that EnviroTech was learning how to selectively portray differences and dependencies in a way that tapped into valued cultural understandings around what counted as valid concerns and how to portray them.

Learning from earlier interactions and the accumulation of assets clearly are not independent of each other. For example, EnviroTech's very use of providing data and offering explanations moves can be seen as evidence of its members' accumulation of normative knowledge – 'how to get things done' – in this setting. Providing data didn't simply represent differences, but it did so in a way that made these differences acceptable and legitimate to the recipients. Recall that Tech's common language was that of data, and that its members were suspicious of claims made without sufficient data. Compared to the Recycler project where differences were represented quite baldly, by appealing to commitments, the moves used on the later projects suggest a more nuanced appreciation of the dominant cultural norms.

A final possibility remains that selling the environmental issues became more effective over time because Tech became more receptive to the issues. While this would not explain the shift in the moves used by EnviroTech (see Table 6.2), it is possible that this is an additional dynamic in the overall story of what changed across the seven projects. While some key members of Tech almost certainly became more aware of environmental issues and the need to address them, perhaps as much through prominent failures such as the Destructors as any other means, it would be hard to support a broader shift in receptivity or a change in Tech's culture that would signal such receptivity. The available evidence suggests that Tech's cultural understandings were reinforced, if changed at all, rather than revised through their experiences with the environmental issues. Recall that those closely involved in the Destructor project concluded that in the future Tech should 'own' the development of equipment for environmental treatment to ensure that it was developed its way. (This change never did come about.) Much later, following the successful completion of the Clean Air project, an EnviroTech manager told the EnviroCouncil that he'd received 'very strong feedback from the [Tech senior management group] that they wanted more solutions like [the Clean Air project]' because of its strong resemblance to mainstream Tech projects – focused, technically oriented, and blind to local differences in environmental regulations or requirements.

CULTURAL CHANGE NOT CULTURE CHANGE

What happened over time as EnviroTech sought to integrate environmental issues more closely with the work of Tech cannot rightly be called 'culture change.' Culture change implies a shift in the pattern of meanings that are salient within a group, and an associated shift in how problems are set and what strategies for action are employed to solve them. This did not occur at Chipco. Tech remained as committed to its cultural understandings as it always had been, orienting itself to address problems that represented critical constraints on manufacturing or new process development (for future manufacturing) and solving these problems with focused, swift and sometimes brute technical force. What *did* happen may be described as 'cultural' change in that it was a culturally consistent way of bringing about change within an existing, dominant pattern of cultural meanings. EnviroTech (and the groups and individuals that preceded it) lacked the capacity to impose change within Chipco. The group held very limited formal power, similarly limited informal power in its interactions with Tech, and operated in an organizational setting in which it played a bit part, at best, in the construction of meaning that was more broadly shared. Under such conditions, EnviroTech became effective only by learning about and selectively activating dominant cultural meanings for what constituted a problem and what constituted a solution.

Like the earlier work on issue selling, this analysis suggests that those who operate from positions of disadvantage in the hierarchical, political and/or cultural structures of their organizations can nonetheless bring about change in whether and how certain issues are addressed. Unlike earlier work on issue selling, this analysis draws attention to the role of cultural meanings and norms, in particular, in both constraining and enabling the actions issue sellers can take to advance their ends. While their assets (or lack thereof) can be very important to an issue seller's potential to influence others, it is the moves they make, and the effect these moves have on others' understandings of the problem, that matter most in practice.

Effective moves trigger issue recipients' attention and action by tapping into their cultural meanings; these moves advance the new issues within the organization by drawing relevant (but not extreme) distinctions between them and 'business as usual.'

This balance between representing difference and dependency, and not too much of either, is not easily struck. The Chipco data suggests that it is acquired over time, through situated encounters that bring the problems of different groups and their respective strategies for action into direct contact. It was through the friction of these encounters that the nature and depth of misrecognition or mistrust of the environmental issues were revealed, as were the norms and interests of the dominant group. The series of repeated encounters, failures and adjustments demonstrate that those working on environmental issues gradually gained competence to operate effectively within Tech's culture, eventually representing the 'new' issues in a way that reveals a nuanced appreciation for dominant modes of problem setting and strategies for action. They did not completely reformulate problems as Tech problems, but carved out those aspects that they could represent as Tech problems and continued to work on other aspects creatively.

In sum, the project analysis shows that selling issues to influence the attention and action of a dominant group involves tapping into and activating the cultural meanings resonant within that group. But issue selling under such circumstances is not a one-off process. It is accumulative, with sellers gaining the capacity to influence others through repeated efforts and experiences. There are three potential mechanisms by which issue selling may change over time, across discrete efforts. First, sellers may accumulate assets over time that enable them to launch moves which tap into the meanings of the more powerful group. Such changes in assets might result from changes in the composition and authority of the group, their expertise, relationships and normative knowledge. Second, sellers may actively adjust their choice of moves based on experiences of failure, resistance, or success in prior selling efforts. Earlier efforts help those advancing the issue to learn about what other groups value, and how they value it. They also act as experiments to probe which moves seem to produce effective outcomes and which do not. Finally, recipient's understandings, and their setting of problems and strategies for action, may change as a result of being exposed to the issue and its implications. The logics associated with each of these mechanisms are, respectively, a logic of accumulation of the capacity to make moves, a logic of learning over time to make 'better' moves, and a logic of 'changing the minds' of the targets of influence. Of course, all three mechanisms may be present, and, if so, will likely interact with each other.

The final mechanism for change – shifting the recipients' cultural understandings so they attend to and act on the issue – is likely the ultimate goal of issue-selling efforts. However, both this analysis and prior research suggest that it may well not be the immediate or even eventual outcome. Sellers often tie their messages to existing organizational goals or values, which can lead to a conservative bias in issue-selling efforts (Dutton *et al.*, 2001; Bansal, 2003) as well as reinforcement of existing cultural understandings. Issue recipients' cultural understandings may be quite durable and in such circumstances change will come more readily by using these understandings for new purposes rather than fundamentally revising them. In the next chapter, I step away from the immediate results from Chipco and put these insights and others into a larger context.

NOTES

1. A modified version of the project analysis appears in J. Howard-Grenville (2007) 'Developing issue selling effectiveness over time: Issue selling as resourcing', *Organization Science* (forthcoming). In that article, the project analysis is used to develop a theoretical argument that issue selling can be seen as a form of resourcing (Feldman, 2004) that is, a practical accomplishment through which issue sellers' moves enact key schemas held by issue recipients, triggering their attention and action on an issue. Issue selling as resourcing builds on recent work on resources and organizational boundaries to address how organizational contexts shape opportunities for and barriers to issue selling and to identify how issue sellers learn to operate effectively within them. In this chapter, the projects are analyzed and the lens of issue selling is used to demonstrate how EnviroTech both learned about Tech's cultural meanings and began to use them to their advantage to frame the environmental issues.
2. For the first I had only two interviews and could not obtain enough other interviews and archival documents to corroborate the information obtained in the interviews. For the second, I had only a few documents and limited observational data, and no interviews. As all the other projects I analyzed in depth had a combination of comprehensive interview, archival and observational data, and typically all three, I felt any analysis of these two projects would not be comparable.
3. Some of the later, successful projects were not completed or even fully implemented at the time of the study, so it would be premature to conclude that they necessarily fully met their goals. They did, however, gain approval and in many cases funding from Tech.
4. The metric here is pounds per wafer start, with a wafer start being the measure of fab throughput. '*xxx*,' '*yyy*' and '*zzz*' refer to numbers that are much smaller than 1, but are specified to several significant digits.
5. 20X indicates a factor of 20 times the emissions goal.
6. This includes only environmental employees with the large Environment, Health and Safety (EH&S) groups. Also, the site environmental employees are only included for the semiconductor fabrication facility sites. There are additional environmental employees for other sites where chip testing and assembly occur.
7. EnviroTech reported into Materials, a group that supported operations in Tech and the Manufacturing fabs.
8. Even relatively common chemicals can be expensive for semiconductor manufacturing use because they have to be prepared to a very high level of purity to reduce contamination.

7. Corporate culture and environmental practice

> The world we see is . . . revealed against a background of belief, without which it could not appear as it does . . . The [environmental] crisis is not simply something we can examine and resolve. We are the environmental crisis.
>
> (Evernden, 1985: 128)

We are the environmental crisis. A reminder of the often invisible but nonetheless intimate connections between modern human activity and environmental degradation? A call for responsibility to be taken for the environmental change wrought by society? Or an existential statement? Evernden implies the latter, writing that 'the crisis is a visible manifestation of our very being' (1985: 128). But there is another way of thinking of this. Crises are departures – often sudden and significant ones – from some expected norm. To know a crisis is to understand at some level the norm. To be sure, crises have their own existence; they are not purely figments of an active imagination or a narrow definition of the norm. In the environmental realm real problems like global climate change, species loss, and ozone depletion go on whether we label them or not. But the exact nature and magnitude of a crisis depends on who is doing the labeling, and the norms they are using for comparison.

Seen this way, the suggestion that we are the environmental crisis demands a closer examination of the 'we.' This book's exploration of a single company and its culture is an attempt to uncover and understand how a modern corporation constructs the environment, the problems or 'crises' it sees, and the prescriptions for action it arrives at. There are many 'we's' of course, even within a single corporation, so an understanding of the actions that are ultimately taken on environmental issues must account for the interpretations of different groups, their interactions, and their relative power.

The essential idea advanced here is that culture – the pattern of meanings and action sustained by members of a group of people – matters a great deal to interpretation and action on environmental issues. It matters because cultures provide categories that help their members discern normality and surprise, and they offer repertoires of strategies for action that are appropriate to the matters of the culture. Corporate cultures are no different; their members select issues for attention, label them problems or crises and act on them accordingly. In doing this, they also exclude certain issues from consideration. Many issues are simply never paid the compliment of being labeled a 'problem' for a company. While cultures do not fully determine their members' actions, the Chipco case demonstrates that they can provide a compelling and largely self-consistent set of meanings and incentives that strongly influence interpretations and actions.

Chipco is an extreme case where, perhaps more so than in any other industry, its manufacturing success relies on maintaining an exquisitely controlled internal environment; its fabs are touted as the cleanest places on earth. The outside should not get in, indeed it would be disastrous if it did. Work is organized to maintain this order, reproduce it across the globe, and make the technological advances needed to continually improve upon it. Environmental demands disrupt this, both directly by posing a potential threat to the maintenance of manufacturing order, and indirectly by showing up as different kinds of problems, and often demanding different kinds of solutions. In other companies one could expect similar tensions to show up between the core culture of the organization, and the demands of environmental work, but the particular manifestations of these tensions would only be evident through a detailed understanding of the work and culture.

The cultural perspective on environmental practice developed in this book has implications for: first, the debate over what shapes corporate environmental management; second, understanding culture, power, interpretation and action within organizations; and finally, for practice and policy aimed at improving corporate environmental management.

GETTING INSIDE ENVIRONMENTAL MANAGEMENT

At Chipco, Tech and EnviroTech were engaged in different work. They not only reported to different management, sat in different cubicles, and attended (largely) different meetings, but they engaged a different physical world, saw knowledge and data differently, and had different degrees of control over how and by whom their work was evaluated. The material properties of silicon – scalability and divisibility – that gave Moore's Law its grounding in physical reality also gave Tech engineers clear and measurable targets for process improvement, and the initial contours of their role specialization. Moore's Law as reproduced by Chipco and others also carved time into discrete chunks and gave engineers confidence in the unfolding of future time and the linear accumulation of process-related knowledge.

EnviroTech and others engaged in environmental work encountered a messier physical world. Its needs and constraints were communicated not in a direct, predictable fashion, but through intermediaries – regulation, community concern, scientific findings. Planning and control were possible in only the near term, but even that was fraught with complexity. Nonetheless, they were participants in Chipco's broader culture, subject to the same pressures for the pursuit of measurable goals, the elimination of technical and operational differences between facilities, and the development and execution of a clear roadmap of their (at least near) future actions.

As a result of these similarities and differences in how each group participated in and recreated a culture of planning, measurement and control within Chipco, the groups saw in environmental issues somewhat different problems to be solved and drew on somewhat different strategies for action to solve them. The company's culture and, in particular, how the culture was distributed within and between groups, strongly shaped how the outside world was viewed, and how particular environmental problems were set and acted upon. For Tech, problems were things that impeded the reliable operation of future manufacturing processes. They could be quantified with data and solved through the application of technical expertise and hard work. EnviroTech learned over time to represent environmental issues in this way, giving up some of the complexity surrounding the issues to gain attention to them and generate action on them. There are at least three critical implications of this cultural viewpoint for understanding corporate environmental practice.

First, the environmental problems addressed by companies are not necessarily problems of all, or even problems of all within an industry, geography, or some other arbitrary external boundary. Environmental issues or pressures may look very similar, but the company itself gets a say in how it constructs an environmental problem. A company's environmental problems are the result of an encounter between the issues or pressures that arise externally, and the internal conditions that shape particular problem interpretations. Others have argued that a variety of internal conditions enter this negotiation, including the perceptions of individual managers, their internal incentives, and even their leadership styles (Prakash, 2000; Gunningham *et al.*, 2003). But one can rightly ask, where do managerial incentives or styles come from? Culture, seen as patterns of meaning and action sustained by their members, captures much of what lies beneath these other internal factors.

The advantage of culture as an explanation for the internal factors that shape interpretations of and actions on external pressures is that, once a culture is understood, one need not peel the onion much further back. Of course, the very advantage of culture here is also the source of its disadvantage. Culture is not easy to understand, it cannot be gleaned from a handful of interviews or a survey. And culture is not like a straightjacket on its members. Individuals can act differently within cultures, perhaps expressing their own personal interpretations of issues more actively than they offer culturally consistent interpretations. But actions on most problems, environmental or otherwise, are collective accomplishments, suggesting that bucking the culturally valued strategies for action can not easily be pulled off by one individual, unless that person has significant influence over the others involved.

This relates to a second implication of explaining corporate environmental practice culturally. Since cultural meanings and actions are not evenly shared within an organization, there is a further internal negotiation that may occur around any given environmental issue. Different groups – like Tech and EnviroTech in Chipco – might come up with quite different problems when faced with an environmental issue. Even if they come up with the same problem, they might have different strategies for action for approaching it. What appears to the outside world as a corporation's action on a given issue may therefore be much more complex than simply the interaction of external pressures with internal cultural understandings, as these understandings themselves may be subject to internal negotiation and contestation.

Finally, by paying attention to culture and its influence on interpretation and action on environmental issues, one also gains a longer term, more dynamic view of internal decision-making. Work that looks only at external signals of corporate environmental practice can be plagued by difficulty in identifying what actually happened, and comparing this adequately across a sample of firms. Does adoption of a voluntary environmental management scheme mean the same thing in all companies? How does one differentiate between formal adoption (a managerial commitment) and actual implementation? Are different facilities within a company at vastly different stages of practice even though they formally have adopted the same environmental practices? Looking as I did at how several environmental projects unfolded over time at a single company reveals that the patterns and paths of implementation are highly consequential to actual actions and outcomes. Beyond the simple observations that some initiatives fail to meet their promises and others evolve in unpredictable ways, the Chipco analysis also suggests that managers and employees actively adjust their approaches based on the success or failure of earlier projects. This kind of analysis can help to tease out more nuanced explanations for whether and how environmental initiatives are implemented and deepen understanding of differences between companies seen to be adopting similar practices.

In sum, a close understanding of a company's culture can strongly complement other explanations for corporate environmental practices. External factors will always be an important part of the explanation, for without the particular types of pressures exerted by regulation, society, competition, and the natural world itself, environmental issues would never show up as they do for companies, nor have the initial contours of the problems they may become for a company. But if scholars never step inside and seek to closely understand the work of the organization, the cultural understandings that are sustained, and the complexities and contradictions within these, then explanations of the environmental problems companies seek to address and their actions to address them will always be incomplete.

CHANGE THROUGH, NOT OF, CULTURE

Despite their imperfect fit with the dominant culture, environmental issues did move somewhat closer to the 'mainstream' at Chipco over the time period that I studied. The success of the later projects suggests that the organization got better at incorporating environmental considerations into manufacturing process development over time. This change represents a kind of culture change, but not of the type hoped for by those who advance the idea that companies will transform their core business in response to environmental pressures (Hunt and Auster, 1990; Roome, 1992; Gladwin *et al.*, 1995; Shrivastava, 1995). At Chipco, Tech's norms for setting and solving problems were holding strong. What changed was EnviroTech's ability to tap into them and use them to advance their ends. By acquiring assets in the form of formal authority, expertise, normative knowledge and relationships, members of EnviroTech gained the capacity to better influence Tech. But more importantly, by adjusting what they actually did – the moves they made – over time and in response to earlier failures, the group learned how to successfully 'sell' environmental issues to Tech and gain action on them.

This kind of change – in how a less powerful group engages the cultural apparatus of a more powerful group – is reminiscent of work on social movements and how they achieve change. Individuals cannot simply appropriate the practices of a dominant group (Creed *et al.*, 2002) but can be active, skillful users of culture (Swidler, 1986: 277). Successful issue selling to advance new issues within organizations may come about through ongoing encounters between groups holding different amounts (and types) of power, and reflection on and adjustment of moves made by the issue sellers over time as a result of these encounters. Skill at reflection and accumulated experience of issue selling may well explain why some issue sellers are more effective than others within the same organization (Dutton *et al.*, 2001). But issue sellers must also remember that recipients' evaluations of their moves are critical to their success and that it may simply take time and repeated interaction to be regarded by recipients as competent and credible. Others have noted that those advancing change from positions of disadvantage often do not have the 'social standing to legitimize their oppositional meanings' but may gain it in a 'piecemeal . . . and often initially provisional' fashion (Steinberg, 1999: 751) over time, and across repeated interactions.

In Chipco's case, the moves used on environmental projects shifted considerably over time as EnviroTech gained the capacity and skill to influence Tech. While the moves on the earliest projects centered on attempting to mimic Tech's strategies for action (for example asserting decision processes, and taking control), those used on the later projects attempted to trigger Tech's meanings for what constituted a 'problem' (for example, through providing data and offering explanations). The latter appropriately represented both differences (in the specialized knowledge and associated criteria used to evaluate it) and dependencies (constraints posed by the work of one group on the other) associated with the issues and made them relevant to the recipients.

There is no 'magic formula' for advancing new issues in this way, however. The details of which patterns of moves will be successful and unsuccessful in other organizations are sure to be different. As others have shown, the same moves may be used on successful and unsuccessful issue selling efforts (Schilit and Paine, 1987; Dutton *et al.*, 2001), suggesting that a single move or even set of moves can have different effects. The moves must be understood in the cultural context in which they are attempted; successful moves will be distinguished from unsuccessful ones based on what they do, not what they are. Regardless of the organization or its dominant cultural categories and meanings, effective patterns of moves likely expose relevant differences and dependencies to tap into recipients' cultural meanings for what constitutes a 'problem'; exactly how they do so must be the subject of close attention to the culture. If we accept that individuals are knowledgeable in their use of an organization's norms, and routines (Feldman, 2004; Howard-Grenville, 2005) and capable of advancing new issues creatively (Meyerson and Scully, 1995; Creed *et al.*, 2002), we can learn a great deal about emergent change by attending to the situated, evolving actions and interactions between unequal groups within a culture.

The suggestion that a less powerful group in a company must gradually appropriate the cultural practices of a dominant group presents a rather bleak outlook for fundamental culture change as companies increasingly address issues of environmental protection or other new issues. Indeed, without actually changing the way a more powerful group within a culture sets problems or acts on them, one may simply get more cultural replication – 'business as usual' solutions for issues that really demand new ways of thinking – rather than culture change. But culture change and replication occur through the same mechanisms, situated actions that either revise or recreate patterns of meaning. There is always the scope for actions on new issues to prompt ongoing reflection on and revision of existing practices. But it is no means guaranteed.

While introducing new issues always holds out the possibility that minds are changed, actions altered, and cultural meanings revised as a result, the more cautious prognosis for culture change presented here is perhaps closer to the reality for many large, complex companies. Rarely has attention to environmental issues radically transformed how organizations operate (Halme, 2002; Newton, 2003) and other new issues are often conservatively advanced (Dutton *et al.*, 2001). However, I would wager that since the time of my study, Chipco has had more success at integrating environmental considerations into its manufacturing technology development, as those advancing the environmental issues have gained experience working with Tech and learned from their earlier encounters. I suspect the problems that gain the most attention and action are still 'Tech' problems, but that more of them are successfully set that way. And ultimately, this should not be seen as a failure of culture change. The natural world, at least that which can be measured and managed, is likely better off for it.

The practical challenge and opportunity for groups in other companies seeking to advance new issues – environmental or otherwise – is to discover, through repeated interactions over time, the pattern of moves that enable them to set problems and engage strategies for action that resonate with and activate the interests of a more powerful group. Along the way they must build and acquire assets – formal authority, interpersonal relationships, expertise and normative knowledge – that enable them to effectively make such moves. As others have noted, persistence and patience may be some of the most valuable assets for those seeking to make this kind of change within their companies (Meyerson and Scully, 1995; Dutton *et al.*, 2001) as failures and adjustments are almost inevitably part of the process. However, opportunism is also essential. When a potential 'crisis' of the type related in Chapter 1 appears, those seeking change will use it to demonstrate to others the value of taking such issues seriously.

Designing for Change?

Is there another way? What happens if we relieve internal issue sellers of the full burden of changing how environmental issues are acted on within their companies? Can't managers create conditions that might be more conducive to such a change? Even in a company like Chipco where strong norms surrounding the work are largely at odds with ways of thinking and acting that are demanded by uncertain environmental issues, whose resolution may take decades not months, is there not a way to deal with both? The problem is not even unique to addressing environmental issues. With today's pace of change in technology, information flow, and consumer tastes, many managers recognize, and management scholars argue, that successful firms must simultaneously act in the present and plan for the future. Those who can both execute well on the goals of today, and explore for the opportunities of tomorrow will be the 'ambidextrous organizations' that pursue both incremental gains and radical, disruptive innovation (O'Reilly and Tushman, 2004). In the environmental realm, this might well involve the 'creative destruction' of aspects of an existing firm's core business (Christensen, 1997) as fundamentally new ways of offering a service or product are developed by breaking from the incremental march of the technologies and resources that characterize traditional industrial processes (Hart, 2005).

Designing and successfully operating an ambidextrous organization in practice, however, is even harder than it sounds. One common approach, following the popular success of IBM's 'skunkworks' approach to developing the personal computer, is to structurally separate those engaged in emerging, risky new businesses from those involved in existing ones. Structural separation may then produce different cultures, processes and criteria for success, with alignment managed only at the senior management level (O'Reilly and Tushman, 2004). Not surprisingly, this often leads to isolation and insufficient integration of the innovative projects with the core business (Birkinshaw and Gibson, 2004). Only through the happy marriage of individuals who are oriented to think and act ambidextrously, managers and peers who support such ambidexterity, and a broader organizational context in which it is encouraged, can the much desired outcome of adaptability coupled with solid execution be produced. The Chipco analysis demonstrates that innovation in the environmental realm is tightly connected to innovation in the core technological trajectory. Absent a radical break in this trajectory, it is very difficult to see how innovation that dramatically alters environmental impact associated with manufacturing could be achieved.

Despite these challenges, however, the idea of ambidexterity raises another possibility for replacing the incremental, bottom-up approach to bringing about change in environmental practices described here. A company that is already ambidextrous in its approach to product or process development would be much more likely than a company like Chipco to pursue such an approach. Indeed, it is hard to imagine that a focused and single-minded approach to pursuing a core technological trajectory could be accompanied by a radical, innovative environmental approach. But breaks from 'business as usual' mindsets will be needed in order to design and produce products and service that deliver substantial environmental benefits. The best most companies today can do is to reduce their environmental *un*sustainability; to pursue sustainability demands a much more radical break from existing patterns (Ehrenfeld, 2007). And, while the culture of many companies supports continuity more than change, there are a number of companies that have successfully culti-vated cultures that embrace change, encourage risk-taking, and enable their employees to continually learn and experiment. This orientation, toward experimentation rather than precedent, has also been identified as an approach to improving regulatory approaches to environmental manage-ment (Marcus, Geffen and Sexton, 2002). It bears further attention as the environmental issues facing companies will become only more complex and demand more creative solutions in the future.

THE BIGGER PICTURE REVISITED

I return now to the complex external conditions, outlined in Chapter 2, that define the broader playing field for semiconductor manufacturers. This industry, while perhaps unique as measured by its historic rates of eco-nomic growth and technological change, also reflects a number of other trends that are helping to reshape how environmental (and related social) demands are reaching companies. Getting the inside view on how and why a company selects issues for attention and how it acts on them can suggest some new ways of understanding the external conditions and how they might be shaped as incentives for improving environmental practice and performance.

First, the analysis in this book supports observations that there can be no single policy instrument suited to all firms (Coglianese and Nash, 2001; Gunningham *et al.*, 2003). Increasingly, regulators seek to shape the behav-ior of firms through the use of various voluntary programs, offering recog-nition, perhaps flexibility in certain aspects of regulatory compliance and technical assistance or other inducements. In return, corporate participants are expected to attain superior environmental performance. Other policy instruments include the use of market-based mechanisms that impose costs on firms who, for example, use less-efficient production processes and emit more pollution. But the costs and benefits associated with these schemes are not uniform. We already know that the particular market, competitive, and social demands a firm faces will alter how it responds to these costs and benefits (Esty and Porter, 1998; Reinhardt, 1999; Aragon-Correa and Sharma, 2002; Gunningham *et al.*, 2003). Seeing environmental problems as informed by a company's culture, as well as by external factors, makes it even more difficult to determine clearly what the costs and benefits of particular voluntary programs may be for particular companies, and hence why any given company might choose to participate or not.

Ironically perhaps, looking at environmental management practice as informed by a company's culture suggests that new, flexible policy instruments actually may be less effective than their highly criticized, rigid precursors. Why? One of the key lessons from the Chipco analysis is that environmental issues became consequential for the dominant group when they could be represented as a critical constraint on current or future manufacturing. And making reference to hard regulatory limits was one of the most reliable ways to frame issues in this way. While many companies, Chipco included, enjoy the flexibility afforded by new regulatory approaches, there is something to be said for reducing uncertainty and establishing a goal to work toward. Environmental issues appeared inherently uncertain for Chipco, and one can argue that with scientific information continually accumulating and environmental effects distant in time and space from their causes, they are experienced similarly by many firms. Policy instruments, as one signal that mediates between the outside world and a company's internal world, are one mechanism that can rein in some of this uncertainty, helping those within firms to make it clear what problems they have to solve, and to represent the consequences of not solving them.

The overview in Chapter 2 also suggested that many more external pressures than simply regulatory policy can influence a company's environmental actions and alternatives. Competitive pressures can lead companies to push for voluntary standards (for example, the limits on PFC and PFOS emissions for the semiconductor manufacturing industry) in order to create a 'level playing field' for all participants, regardless of their regulatory jurisdiction. This kind of action may become increasingly important with the globalization of manufacturing as European and, to a lesser degree, North American governments tend to introduce more stringent environmental regulation sooner than their counterparts in other parts of the world. There may be significant incentives for companies operating in these countries to initiate actions that bind all of their competitors to the same standards. But equally important may be internal perceptions of the need for certainty and control, the role of industry-established voluntary targets in providing these, and the fit of such approaches with internal strategies for action. The cultural perspective adds some new ways of thinking about a long-standing debate on who joins or initiates voluntary agreements and why. Is it the 'dirtiest' companies who have the most to gain by improving their image as environmentally proactive? Or is it the industry leaders who have the most to lose if their competitors either operate to different standards or sully the reputation of the entire industry through poor performance or worse, accidents or spills? The answer is not categorical. Other research supports the idea that internal factors strongly condition the decisions of individual companies to participate in programs that allow them to set their own goals and receive recognition (Howard-Grenville *et al.*, 2006). The value of certainty, environmental leadership and recognition are perceived very differently by different firms. Voluntary agreements are here to stay and will always provide an attractive alternative to regulatory approaches. But like regulation, they will never be one-size-fits-all.

Finally, market and social trends continue to redefine externally what counts as environmental responsibility. Some consumers now pay attention to the environmental attributes of a product, rather than just the environmental performance of the processes through which it was manufactured. Broader social awareness of environmental issues, particularly the salient issues of energy consumption and climate change, affects employees, not just 'the public.' In other words, environmental issues are being brought to companies through new and diverse channels, and this is a trend we can expect to continue. Marketing, sales and product development teams, no doubt, have or will soon begin to hear new demands. Employees across all job functions may start to think differently about waste production and energy consumption in their daily work lives. As a result, the sheer number and variety of challenges to a company's established ways of working and core culture will increase, opening up the possibility that change may be brought about in many areas through the culture, not necessarily of it.

At some point, adjustments to what counts as a problem and increasingly frequent actions on 'new' problems may result in broader changes of a company's culture – the patterns of meanings and actions that support them. Whether such a tipping point exists, where it lies within different corporate cultures, how it relates to external triggers and trends, and how to get to it remain larger questions. But it is certain that external and (even gradual) internal change will occur. A key message of this book is that they do not necessarily occur hand-in-hand. Internal corporate cultures are deep and broad; they accumulate over years, often decades, of responsiveness to external conditions, choices of leaders, and actions of myriad members. It would be rash to think they could change overnight, or without reasserting themselves, just because one reading of the natural world demanded it. It is realistic, and necessary, however, to treat them as tools for change and to expect this change to be, by and large, gradual and accumulative, like the workings of culture itself.

CLOSING THOUGHTS

Two months into my time at Chipco, I volunteered to visit a fourth-grade classroom for National Engineers Week. At the end of our hands-on project (instructing an imaginary microprocessor chip to make a real peanut butter sandwich) I asked the class to guess what kind of engineer I was. Several guessed I was a computer engineer. One boy suggested that I did what his Dad did, which had something (he wasn't quite sure what) to do with Chipco's latest product. When I told them I worked as an environmental engineer I heard murmurs of surprise, perhaps disappointment. Then came the questions.

'Do you work outside?' one young girl asked. I was at first taken aback by her strange question. Where did she get such an idea? I then realized that, in the mind of a fourth-grader, an environmental engineer might very well spend her days standing knee-deep in a stream, clad in hip waders, taking water samples and checking up on the state of the flora and fauna. After all, we tend to think of the environment as 'out there' and working on it could well mean working in it. I explained that at Chipco and other manufacturing companies environmental engineers generally work inside to make sure that whatever waste leaves the factory is sufficiently clean.

This question, and its answer, were rather simple compared to others that followed: 'what is an example of the kind of waste you clean up?' and 'where does Chipco's waste go?' Since the school I was visiting was only about four miles from the fab I was acutely aware of how I answered. I found myself explaining that because of the work of environmental engineers, the waste becomes really very clean and then some of it makes its way into the air or the sewer system. I felt myself becoming defensive although I knew that the children had nothing to fear about the fab. I tried to emphasize that my job was about finding ways to reduce the waste, or to recycle chemicals so they could be used again. But I knew that the real situation was far from this simple; environmental work was always about trying to balance between internal norms and external demands.

I was relieved when one girl asked me what else happened at the Chipco site I worked at. This, I thought, was easy. I explained that the engineers developed new techniques for making chips that can run faster and more powerful computers. For example, I mentioned, they have to figure out how to make the 'wires' on a chip even thinner than they were (which, I added, was less than one five-hundredth the width of a human hair). 'Wow,' came the collective response.

As I drove back to the fab, I found myself thinking how much easier it would have been just to talk to the fourth grade about the amazing technical aspects of chip production, rather than raising the taboo and difficult subjects of pollution. But that, I reminded myself, would not have been the whole story.

The symbolic separation of related things is an important accomplishment of cultures, and of individuals. It enables us to make sense of the world and act within its otherwise baffling complexity. But, like any other representations, the separation of work and nature, or of production and pollution, leave blind spots. Fortunately, we have many groups and cultures – corporate and otherwise – to contribute many incomplete representations that may, when pieced together, give a more complete picture. Unfortunately, on the issue of environmental protection, nature itself does not get a say; it relies on us, collectively, to interpret and represent its best interests. Is it robust or fragile, threatened or thriving? These judgments have important consequences for action. As historian William Cronon writes, 'the struggle to live rightly in the world is finally not just about right actions, but about the ideas that lie behind those actions . . . To protect the nature that is all around us, we must think long and hard about the nature we carry inside our heads' (1996: 22).

The aim of this book has been to map out the 'nature' that one company's members carry inside their heads, as a result of the work they do and the way they do it. One lesson that we cannot lose sight of is that nature is inherently contested ground, and will remain so. In our efforts to act rightly we must, at a minimum, continue the conversation, and attend to the debates that ensue. For in attending to these distinctions and differences, we find the openings for change.

Bibliography

Allaire, Y. and M. Firsirotu (1984), 'Theories of organizational culture,' *Organization Studies*, **5** (3), 193–226.

Andersson, L. M. and T. S. Bateman (2000), 'Individual environmental initiative: championing natural environmental issues in US business organizations,' *Academy of Management Journal*, **43** (4), 548–70.

Aragon-Correa, J. A. and S. Sharma (2003), 'A contingent resource-based view of proactive environmental strategy,' *Academy of Management Review*, **28** (1), 71–88.

Ashford, S., N. Rothbard, S. Piderit and J. Dutton (1998), 'Out on a limb: the role of context and impression management in selling gender issues,' *Administrative Science Quarterly*, 43, 23–57.

Ausubel, J. H. (1996), 'The liberation of the environment,' *Daedalus*, **125** (3), 1–17.

Bacharach, S. and M. Baratz (1963), 'Decision and nondecisions: an analytical framework,' *American Political Science Review*, 57, 641–51.

Bansal, P. (2003), 'From issues to actions: the importance of individual concerns and organizational values in responding to natural environment issues,' *Organization Science*, **14** (5), 510–25.

Bansal, P. and J. Gao (2006), 'Building the future by looking to the past: examining research published on organizations and environment,' *Organization & Environment*, **19** (4), 1–21.

Barney, J. (1986), 'Organizational culture: can it be a source of sustained competitive advantage,' *Academy of Management Review*, 11, 656–65.

Barney, J. (1991), 'Firm resources and sustained competitive advantage,' *Journal of Management*, **17** (1), 99–120.

Bechky, B. A. (2003), 'Shared meanings across occupational communities: the transformation of understanding on a production floor,' *Organization Science*, 14, 312–30.

Benford, R. D. and D. A. Snow (2000), 'Framing processes and social movements: an overview and assessment,' *Annual Review of Sociology*, 26, 611–39.

Birkinshaw, J. and C. Gibson (2004), 'Building ambidexterity into an organization,' *MIT Sloan Management Review*, **45** (4), 47–55.

Bloor, G. and P. Dawson (1994), 'Understanding professional culture in organizational context,' *Organization Studies*, **15** (2), 275–95.

Brass, D. and M. Burkhardt (1993), 'Potential power and power use: an investigation of structure and behavior,' *Academy of Management Journal*, **36** (3), 441–70.

Brumfiel, G. (2004), 'Chipping in,' *Nature*, 431, 622–3.

Carlile, P. R. (2002), 'A pragmatic view of knowledge and boundaries: boundary objects in new product development,' *Organizational Science*, 13, 442–55.

Carlile, P. R. (2004), 'Transferring, translating, and transforming: an integrative framework for managing knowledge across boundaries,' *Organization Science*, **15** (5), 555–68.

Carlile, P. R. and E. S. Rebentisch (2003), 'Into the black box: the knowledge transformation cycle,' *Management Science*, **49** (9), 1180–95.

Christmann, P. (2000), 'Effects of "best practices" of environmental management on cost advantage: the role of complementary assets,' *Academy of Management Journal*, **43** (4), 663–80.

Christensen, C. M. (1997), *Innovator's Dilemma: When New Technologies Cause Great Firms to Fail*, Cambridge, MA: Harvard Business School Press Books.

Coglianese, C. (2001), 'Social movements, law, and society: the institutionalization of the environmental movement,' *University of Pennsylvania Law Review*, **150** (1), 85–118.

Coglianese, C. and J. Nash (eds) (2001), *Regulating from the Inside: Can Environmental Management Systems Achieve Policy Goals?* Washington, DC: Resources for the Future.

Coglianese, C. and J. Nash (2002), 'Policy options for improving environmental management in the private sector,' *Environment*, **44** (9), 11–23.

Crane, A. (2000), 'Corporate greening as amoralization,' *Organization Studies*, **21** (4), 673–96.

Creed, W., M. Scully and J. Austin (2002), 'Clothes make the person? The tailoring of legitimating accounts and the social construction of identity,' *Organization Science*, **13** (5), 475–96.

Cronon, W. (1996), 'Introduction: in search of nature,' in W. Cronon (ed.), *Uncommon Ground: Rethinking the Human Place in Nature*, New York: W. W. Norton and Company, pp. 23–56.

Dacin, M., M. Ventresca and B. Beal (1999), 'The embeddedness of organizations: dialogue and directions,' *Journal of Management*, 25, 317–56.

DiMaggio, P. (1991), 'Constructing an organizational field as a professional project: US art museums, 1920–1940,' in W. Powell and P. DiMaggio (eds), *The New Institutionalism in Organizational Analysis*, Chicago, IL: University of Chicago Press, pp. 267–92.

Dougherty, D. (1992), 'Interpretive barriers to successful product innovation in large firms,' *Organization Science*, 3, 179–202.

Douglas, M. (1966), *Purity and Danger: An Analysis of Concepts of Pollution and Taboo*, New York: Praeger.

Douglas, M. (1972), 'Environments at risk,' in J. Benthall (ed.), *Ecology: The Shaping Enquiry*, London: Longman.

Douglas, M. (1978), 'Cultural bias,' Royal Anthropological Institute of Great Britain and Ireland occasional paper no. 35, London.

Douglas, M. (1992), 'A credible biosphere,' in M. Douglas, *Risk and Blame: Essays in Cultural Theory*, New York: Routledge.

Dutton, J. and S. Ashford (1993), 'Selling issues to top management,' *Academy of Management Review*, 18, 397–410.

Dutton, J., S. Ashford, K. Lawrence and K. Miner-Rubino (2002), 'Red light, green light: making sense of the organizational context for issue selling,' *Organization Science*, 13, 355–69.

Dutton, J., S. Ashford, R. O'Neill and K. Lawrence (2001), 'Moves that matter: issue selling and organizational change,' *Academy of Management Journal*, **44** (4), 716–36.

Dutton, J., S. Ashford, E. Wierba, R. O'Neil and E. Hayes (1997), 'Reading the wind: how middle managers assess the context for issue selling to top managers,' *Strategic Management Journal*, 15, 407–25.

eBay (2006) 'Rethink,' http://rethink.ebay.com/odcs/custom.htm?template =ewaste.

Edelman, L., C. Uggen and H. Erlanger (1999), 'The endogeneity of legal regulation: grievance procedures as rational myth,' *American Journal of Sociology*, 105, 406–54.

Egri, C. P. and S. Herman (2000), 'Leadership in the North American environmental sector: values, leadership styles, and contexts of environmental leaders and their organizations,' *Academy of Management Journal*, **43** (4), 571–604.

Ehrenfeld, J. (1997), 'The importance of LCAs – warts and all,' *Journal of Industrial Ecology*, **1** (2), 41–50.

Eisenhardt, K. M. (1989), 'Building theories from case study research,' *Academy of Management Review*, **14** (4), 532–50.

Elrod, S. and W. Worth (2000), 'Environment, safety and health,' in Y. Nishi and R. Doering (eds), *Handbook of Semiconductor Manufacturing Technology*, New York: Marcel Dekker.

EPA (US Environmental Protection Agency) (2003), 'Toxics release inventory,' accessed at www.epa.gov/tri-efdr/.

EPA (US Environmental Protection Agency) (1999), '1997 toxics release inventory,' Public Data Release Report, accessed at www.epa.gov/opptintr/tri/tri97/drhome.htm.

Esty, D. C. and M. E. Porter (1998), 'Industrial ecology and competitiveness: strategic implications for the firm,' *Journal of Industrial Ecology*, **2** (1), 35–43.

Evernden, N. (1985), *The Natural Alien*, Toronto: University of Toronto Press.

Feldman, M. S. (2004), 'Resources in emerging structures and processes of change,' *Organization Science*, **15** (3), 295–309.

Fligstein, N. (1997), 'Social skill and institutional theory,' *American Behavioral Scientist*, **40** (4), 397–405.

Fligstein, N. (2001), 'Social skill and the theory of fields,' *Sociological Theory*, **19** (2), 105–25.

Forbes, L. C. and J. M. Jermier (2002), 'The institutionalization of voluntary organizational greening and the ideals of environmentalism: lessons about official culture from symbolic organization theory,' in A. J. Hoffman and M. J. Ventresca (eds), *Organizations, Policy and the Natural Environment*, Stanford, CA: Stanford University Press, pp. 194–213.

Frank, D., A. Hironaka and E. Schofer (2000), 'The nation-state and the natural environment over the twentieth century,' *American Sociological Review*, **65** (1), 96–116.

Friedman, M. (1970), 'The social responsibility of business is to increase its profits,' *The New York Times Magazine*, 13 September, pp. 32–33, 122, 124, 126.

Geertz, C. (1973), 'Thick description: toward an interpretive theory of culture,' in C. Geertz, *The Interpretation of Cultures*, New York: Basic Books, pp. 3–30.

Giddens, A. (1984), *The Constitution of Society: Outline of the Theory of Structure*, Berkeley, CA: University of California Press.

Giddens, A. (1993), *New Rules of Sociological Method*, Stanford, CA: Stanford University Press.

Gladwin, T. N., J. J. Kennelly and T. S. Krauss (1995), 'Shifting paradigms for sustainable development: implications for management theory and research,' *Academy of Management Review*, **20** (4), 874–907.

Glaser, B. G. and A. L. Strauss (1967), *The Discovery of Grounded Theory: Strategies for Qualitative Research*, New York: Aldine de Gruyter.

Goffman, E. (1981), *Forms of Talk*, Philadelphia, PA: University of Pennsylvania Press.

Golden, B. (1992), 'The past is the past – or is it? The use of retrospective accounts as indicators of past strategy,' *Academy of Management Journal*, 35, 848–60.

Graedel, T. (1997), 'The grand objectives: a framework for prioritized grouping of environmental concerns in life-cycle assessment,' *Journal of Industrial Ecology*, **1** (2), 51–64.

Graedel, T. and J. Howard-Grenville (2005), *Greening the Industrial Facility: Perspectives, Approaches, and Tools*, New York: Springer.

Greenwood, R., R. Suddaby and C. Hinings (2002), 'Theorizing change: the role of professional associations in the transformation of institutionalized fields,' *Academy of Management Journal*, **45** (1), 58–80.

Gregory, K. (1983), 'Native-view paradigms: multiple cultures and culture conflict in organizations,' *Administrative Science Quarterly*, **28** (3), 359–76.

Gunningham, N., R. Kagan and D. Thornton (2003), *Shades of Green: Business, Regulation, and Environment*, Stanford, CA: Stanford University Press.

Halme, M. (2002), 'Corporate environmental paradigms in shift: learning during the course of action at UPM-Kymmene,' *Journal of Management Studies*, **39** (8), 1087–109.

Hansen, M. T. (1999), 'The search-transfer problem: the role of weak ties in sharing knowledge across organization subunits,' *Administrative Science Quarterly*, **44** (1), 82–111.

Hardy, C. (1994), 'Power and politics in organizations,' in C. Hardy (ed.), *Managing Strategic Action*, Thousand Oaks, CA: Sage Publications, pp. 220–38.

Hart, S. (1995), 'A natural-resource based view of the firm,' *Academy of Management Review*, **20** (4), 986–1014.

Hart, S. (2005), *Capitalism at the Crossroads: The Unlimited Business Opportunities in Solving the World's Most Difficult Problems*, Upper Saddle River, NJ: Wharton School Publishing.

Hickson, D., C. Hinings, R. Lee, R. Schenck and J. Pennings (1971), 'A structural contingencies theory of intraorganizational power,' *Administrative Science Quarterly*, **16** (2), 216–29.

Hinings, C., D. Hickson, J. Pennings and R. Schenck (1974), 'Structural conditions of intraorganizational power,' *Administrative Science Quarterly*, **19** (1), 22–44.

Hobbes, T. (1651 [1985]), *Leviathan*, edited by C. Macpherson, London: Penguin Books.

Hoffman, A. J. (1999), 'Institutional evolution and change: environmentalism and the US chemical industry,' *Academy of Management Journal*, **42** (4), 351–71.

Hoffman, A. J. (2001), *From Heresy to Dogma: An Institutional History of Corporate Environmentalism*, Stanford, CA: Stanford University Press.

Hoffman, A. J. (2006), 'Getting ahead of the curve: corporate strategies that address climate change,' report prepared for the Pew Center on Global Climate Change, October 2006, acessed at www.pewclimate.org/global-warming-in-depth/all_reports/corporate_strategies/index.cfm.

Hofstede, G. (1998), 'Identifying organizational subcultures: an empirical approach,' *Journal of Management Studies*, **35** (1), 1–12.

Horrigan, J., F. Irwin and E. Cook (1998), *Taking a Byte out of Carbon*, Washington, DC: World Resources Institute.

Howard, J., J. Nash and J. Ehrenfeld (2000), 'Standard or smokescreen: implementation of a voluntary environmental code,' *California Management Review*, **42** (2), 63–82.

Howard-Grenville, J. (2005), 'The persistence of flexible organizational routines: the role of agency and organizational context,' *Organization Science*, **18** (1), 618–36.

Howard-Grenville, J. (2007), 'Developing issue selling effectiveness over time: issue selling as resourcing,' *Organization Science* (forthcoming).

Howard-Grenville, J. and A. J. Hoffman (2003), 'The importance of cultural framing to the success of social initiatives in business,' *Academy of Management Executive*, **17** (2), 70–84.

Howard-Grenville, J., A. Hoffman and C. Bhattacharya (2007), 'Who can act on sustainability issues? Corporate capital and the configuration of organizational fields as enablers,' in S. Sharma, M. Starik and B. Husted (eds), *Organizations and the Sustainability Mosaic: Crafting Long-Term Ecological and Societal Solutions*, Cheltenham, UK and Northampton, US: Edward Elgar.

Howard-Grenville, J., J. Nash and C. Coglianese (2006), 'Constructing the license to operate: internal factors and their influence on corporate environmental decisions,' University of Pennsylvania Law School Scholarship at Penn Law paper 105, accessed at http://lsr.nellco.org/upenn/wps/papers/105.

Hunt, C. and E. Auster (1990), 'Proactive environmental management: avoiding the toxic trap,' *Sloan Management Review*, **31** (2), 7–18.

Jaffe, A., S. Peterson and R. Stavins (1995), 'Environmental regulation and the competitiveness of US manufacturing: what does the evidence tell us,' *Journal of Economic Literature*, **33** (1), 132–63.

Jermier, J., J. Slocum, L. Fry and J. Gaines (1991), 'Organizational subcultures in a soft bureaucracy: resistance behind the myth and façade of an official culture,' *Organization Science*, **2** (2), 170–94.

Kipinis, D., S. Schmidt and I. Wilkinson (1980), 'Intraorganizational influence tactics: explorations in getting one's way,' *Journal of Applied Psychology*, 65, 440–52.

Kirschner, E. (1995), 'Chemical industry modernizes aging plants for safety and efficiency,' *Chemical and Engineering News*, 10 July, pp. 14–18.

KPMG (2005), *KPMG International Survey of Corporate Responsibility Reporting 2005*, accessed at www.kpmg.com/About/IAR2005/Further Reading/CSRSurvey.htm.

Kunda, G. (1992), *Engineering Culture: Control and Commitment in a High-Tech Corporation*, Philadelphia, PA: Temple University Press.

Lawrence, P. R. and J. W. Lorsch (1967), 'Differentiation and integration in complex organizations,' *Administrative Science Quarterly*, **12** (1), 1–47.

Locke, J. (1690 [1996]), *Two Treatises of Government*, edited by W. Carpenter, London: J. M. Dent & Sons.

Lukes, S. (1974), *Power: A Radical View*, London: Macmillan.

Maguire, S., C. Hardy and T. Lawrence (2004), 'Institutional entrepreneurship in emerging fields: HIV/AIDS treatment advocacy in Canada,' *Academy of Management Journal*, **47** (5), 657–79.

Mahoney, R. (1996), *Beyond Empowerment: Relevant Ad Hockery*, Center for the Study of American Business CEO Series no. 1, Washington University, St Louis, MO.

Malone, M. (1998), 'To infinity and beyond,' in R. Smolan and J. Erwitt (eds), *One Digital Day*, New York: Times Books, pp. 115–20.

Marcus, A. and M. Nichols (1999), 'On the edge: heeding the warnings of unusual events,' *Organization Science*, **10** (4), 482–99.

Marcus, A., D. Geffen and K. Sexton (2002), *Reinventing Environmental Regulation: Lessons from Project XL*, Washington, DC: Resources for the Future.

Margolis, J. D. and J. P. Walsh (2003), 'Misery loves companies: rethinking social initiatives in business,' *Administrative Science Quarterly*, 48, 268–305.

Martin, J. (2002), *Organizational Culture: Mapping the Terrain*, Thousand Oaks, CA: Sage Publications.

McKibben, B. (1990), *The End of Nature*, New York: Penguin Books.

MECS (Manufacturing Energy Consumption Survey) (2002), 'Energy information administration,' US Department of Energy, accessed at www.eia.doe.gov/emeu/mecs/mecs 2002/data02/shelltables.html.

Meyerson, D. and J. Martin (1987), 'Cultural change: an integration of three different views,' *Journal of Management Studies*, **24** (6), 623–47.

Meyerson, D. and M. Scully (1995), 'Tempered radicalism and the politics of ambivalence and change,' *Organization Science*, **6** (5), 585–600.

Miles, M. B. and A. M. Huberman (1994), *Qualitative Data Analysis: An Expanded Sourcebook*, 2nd edn, Thousand Oaks, CA: Sage Publications.

Moore, G. E. (1965), 'Cramming more components onto integrated circuits,' *Electronics*, **38** (8), 114–17.

Murphy, C., G. Kenig, D. Allen, J. Laurent and D. Dyer (2003), 'Development of parametric material, energy, and emission inventories for wafer fabrication in the semiconductor industry,' *Environmental Science and Technology*, **37** (23), 5373–82.

National Academy of Sciences (1999), *Industrial Environmental Performance Metrics: Challenges and Opportunities*, Washington, DC: National Academies Press.

Newton, T. J. (2003), 'Creating the new ecological order? Elias and actor-network theory,' *Academy of Management Review*, **27** (4), 523–40.

Oliver, P. (1991), 'Strategic responses to institutional processes,' *Academy of Management Review*, 16, 145–79.

O'Reilly, C. and M. Tushman (2004), 'The ambidextrous organization,' *Harvard Business Review*, **82** (4), 74–81.

Pearce, L. (ed.) (2005), 'Semiconductors and related devices,' in *Encyclopedia of American Industries Volume 1: Manufacturing Industries*, 4th edn, Detroit, MI, pp. 1085–91.

Pentland, B. (1992), 'Organizing moves in software support hot lines,' *Administrative Science Quarterly*, **37** (4), 527–48.

Perrow, C. (1972), *Complex Organizations: A Critical Essay*, Chicago, IL: Scott Foresman.

Pettigrew, A. M. (1990), 'Longitudinal field research on change: theory and practice,' *Organization Science*, **1** (3), 267–92.

Phillips, N. (1997), 'Bringing the organization back in: a comment on conceptualizations of power in upward influence,' *Journal of Organizational Behavior*, 18, 43–7.

Porter, M. E., and C. van der Linde (1995), 'Toward a new conception of the environment-competitiveness relationship,' *Journal of Economic Perspectives*, **9** (4), 97–118.

Powell, W. and P. DiMaggio (eds) (1991), *The New Institutionalism in Organizational Analysis*, Chicago, IL: University of Chicago Press.

Prakash, A. (2000), *Greening the Firm: The Politics of Corporate Environmentalism*, Cambridge, UK: Cambridge University Press.

Ranson, S., B. Hinings and R. Greenwood (1980), 'The structuring of organizational structures,' *Administrative Science Quarterly*, **25** (1), 1–14.

Reinhardt, F. (1999), 'Market failure and the environmental policies of firms: economic rationales for "beyond compliance" behavior,' *Journal of Industrial Ecology*, **3** (1), 9–21.

Resetar, S. (1999), *Technology Forces at Work: Profiles of Environmental Research and Development at Dupont, Intel, Monsanto, and Xerox*, Washington, DC: RAND.

Riley, P. (1983), 'A structurationist account of political culture,' *Administrative Science Quarterly*, **28** (3), 414–37.

Roome, N. (1992), 'Developing environmental management strategies,' *Business Strategy and the Environment*, **1** (1), 11–23.

Russo, M. V. and P. Fouts (1997), 'A resource-based perspective on corporate environmental performance and profitability,' *Academy of Management Journal*, **40** (3), 534–59.

Schein, E. H. (1992), *Organizational Culture and Leadership*, 2nd edn, San Francisco, CA: Jossey-Bass.

Schein, E. H. (1996), 'Culture: The missing concept in organization studies,' *Administrative Science Quarterly*, **41** (2), 229–40.

Schein, E. H. (1996), 'Three cultures of management: the key to organizational learning,' *Sloan Management Review*, **38** (1), 9–20.

Schilit, W. K. and F. T. Paine (1987), 'An examination of the underlying dynamics of strategic decisions subject to upward influence activity,' *Journal of Management Studies*, 24, 161–87.

Schön, D. A. (1983), *The Reflective Practitioner*, New York: Basic Books.

Scott, W. R. (1995), *Institutions and Organizations*, Thousand Oaks, CA: Sage Publications.

Semiconductor Industry Association (2006a), 'SIA issue backgrounders: occupational health and safety,' accessed at www.sia-online.org/backgrounders_ohs.cfm.

Semiconductor Industry Association (2006b), 'Total semiconductor world market sales and shares 1982–2005,' accessed at www.sia-online.org/pre_stat.cfm?ID=179.

Semiconductor Industry Association (2006c), 'SICAS Capacity and Utilization Rates Q2 2006,' accessed at www.sia-online.org/pre_stat.cfm?ID= 296.

Semiconductor Industry Association (2006d), 'SIA Issue Backgrounders: Keeping Semiconductor Leadership in the US,' accessed at www.sia-online. org/backgrounders_Semiconductor_Leadership.cfm.

Semiconductor Industry Association (2006e), 'PFOS reduction agreement,' press release, accessed at www.sia-online.org/pre_stat.cfm?ID= 294.

Sewell, W. H. (1992), 'A theory of structure: duality, agency, and transformation,' *American Journal of Sociology*, **98** (1), 1–27.

Sharma, S. (2000), 'Managerial interpretations and organizational context as predictors of corporate choice of environmental strategy,' *Academy of Management Journal*, **43** (4), 681–97.

Sharma, S. and H. Vredenburg (1998), 'Proactive corporate environmental strategy and the development of competitively valuable organizational capabilities,' *Strategic Management Journal*, 19, 729–53.

Shrivastava, P. (1995), 'Ecocentric management in a risk society,' *Academy of Management Review*, **20** (1), 118–37.

Smircich, L. (1983), 'Concepts of culture and organizational analysis,' *Administrative Science Quarterly*, **28** (3), 339–58.

Smith, V. (1990), *Managing in the Corporate Interest: Control and Resistance in an American Bank*, Berkeley, CA: University of California Press.

Smith-Doerr, L. and W. W. Powell (2005), 'Networks and economic life,' in N. J. Smelser and R. Swedberg (eds), *The Handbook of Economic Sociology*, 2nd edn, Princeton, NJ: Sage/Princeton University Press.

Starkey, K. and A. Crane (2003), 'Toward green narrative: management and the evolutionary epic,' *Academy of Management Review*, **28** (2), 220–37.

Steinberg, M. (1999), 'The talk and back talk of collective action: a dialogic analysis of repertoires of discourse among nineteenth-century English cotton spinners,' *American Journal of Sociology*, **105** (3), 736–80.

Stevenson, W. and J. Bartunek (1996), 'Power, interaction, position, and the generation of cultural agreement in organizations,' *Human Relations*, **49** (1), 75–104.

Swidler, A. (1986), 'Culture in action: symbols and strategies,' *American Sociological Review*, **51** (2), 273–86.

Thompson, M., R. Ellis and A. Wildavsky (1990), *Cultural Theory*, Boulder, CO: Westview Press.

Toffel, M. and A. Horvath (2004), 'Environmental implications of wireless technologies: news delivery and business meetings,' *Environmental Science and Technology*, **38** (11), 2961–70.

US Department of Commerce (1986), *1982 Census of Manufactures: Water Use in Manufacturing*, Washington, DC: Bureau of the Census.

US Department of Commerce (1994), *1994 Annual Survey of Manufactures: Statistics for Industry Groups and Industries*, Washington, DC: Bureau of the Census.

US Department of Commerce (1996), *1996 Annual Survey of Manufactures: Statistics for Industry Groups and Industries*, Washington, DC: Bureau of the Census.

Van Maanen, J. and S. R. Barley (1985), 'Cultural organization: fragments of a theory,' in P. J. Frost, L. F. Moore, M. R. Louis, C. C. Lundberg and J. Martin (eds), *Organization Culture*, Newbury Park, CA: Sage Publications, pp. 31–53.

Van Maanen, J. (1988), *Tales of the Field: On Writing Ethnography*, Chicago, IL: University of Chicago Press.

Waste Online (2006), 'Electrical and electronic equipment recycling information sheet,' accessed at www.wasteonline.org.uk/resources/InformationSheets/ElectricalElectronic.htm.

Weeks, J. (2004), *Unpopular Culture: The Ritual of Complaint in a British Bank, Chicago*, IL: University of Chicago Press.

Weeks, J. and C. Galunic (2003), 'A theory of the cultural evolution of the firm: the intra-organizational ecology of memes,' *Organization Studies*, **24** (8), 1309–52.

Wernerfelt, B. (1984), 'A resource-based view of the firm,' *Strategic Management Journal*, **5** (2), 171–80.

White, R. (1996), 'Are you an environmentalist or do you work for a living: work and nature,' in W. Cronon (ed.), *Uncommon Ground: Rethinking the Human Place in Nature*, New York: W. W. Norton & Company, pp. 171–85.

Williams, E. (2003), 'Forecasting material and economic flows in the global production chain for silicon,' *Technological Forecasting and Social Change*, **70** (4), 341–57.

Williams, E., R. Ayres and M. Heller (2002), 'The 1.7 kilogram microchip: energy and material use in the production of semiconductor devices,' *Environmental Science and Technology*, **36** (24), 5504–10.

Williams, R. (1980), 'Ideas of nature,' in R. Williams (ed.), *Problems in Materialism and Culture*, London: Verso, pp. 67–85.

World Semiconductor Council (1999), 'Position paper regarding PFC emissions reduction goal,' accessed at www.semiconductorcouncil.org/news/agreement.php?rowid=1.

Yukl, G. and C. Falbe (1990), 'Influence tactics in upward, downward, and lateral influence attempts,' *Journal of Applied Psychology*, 75, 416–23.

Index